Ron Foy

Sept 1968

THE ESSENTIALS OF DEMOCRACY

WILLIAM J. COOPER FOUNDATION LECTURES

THE ESSENTIALS
OF DEMOCRACY

BY
A. D. LINDSAY

SECOND EDITION

OXFORD
AT THE CLARENDON PRESS

Oxford University Press, Ely House, London W. 1

GLASGOW   NEW YORK   TORONTO   MELBOURNE   WELLINGTON
CAPE TOWN   SALISBURY   IBADAN   NAIROBI   LUSAKA   ADDIS ABABA
BOMBAY   CALCUTTA   MADRAS   KARACHI   LAHORE   DACCA
KUALA LUMPUR   HONG KONG   TOKYO

First Edition 1929
Second Impression 1930
Second Edition 1935
Second Impression 1940
Third Impression (Reset) 1945
Fourth Impression 1948
Fifth Impression 1952
Sixth Impression 1967

SIXTH IMPRESSION
REPRINTED LITHOGRAPHICALLY IN GREAT BRITAIN
AT THE UNIVERSITY PRESS, OXFORD
BY VIVIAN RIDLER
PRINTER TO THE UNIVERSITY

PREFACE

THESE lectures were given on the William J. Cooper Foundation at Swarthmore College, Pennsylvania, in January of this year. They raise, I am well aware, questions whose proper treatment demands a much longer discussion than the limit of five lectures allowed. But to meet that demand would be to go far beyond their original intention and to expand them into a treatise on the theory of the state; and I have printed them much as they were delivered.

A. D. LINDSAY

July 1929

PREFACE TO THE SECOND EDITION

SINCE these lectures were delivered in 1929 we have witnessed the world-wide economic crisis of 1931 and the Nazi Revolution. The latter event has made a sentence on page 8 about the new democracy of Germany sadly out of date. The economic crisis put a severe strain upon postwar democracy and the new European democracies have mostly succumbed to it; but England and, much more strikingly, America have shown that a democratic government can survive a crisis. The chief moral of the Nazi revolution for the student of democracy is that Germany has set forth with German thoroughness the real nature of the alternative to democracy. Fascist Italy and Bolshevist Russia had already made us talk of the totalitarian state, but neither Italy nor Russia have worked out its implications with the same relentlessness as has National Socialist Germany. The main thesis of these lectures is that discussion is fundamental to democracy: that the purpose of democratic machinery is to represent differences: that democracy requires an official and encouraged opposition: that the principle of toleration is essential to it, and that finally democratic politics can only be successful in a democratic society—and that that means a society of democratic non-political associations. It is pointed out that one implication of all this is that in a democracy politics are a secondary matter, for the purpose of the compulsory machinery of the state is to safeguard and harmonize a common life which has its inspiration in voluntary non-political activities. There can therefore be no compromise between the totalitarian state and democracy. This contrast between the two ways of organizing men: mass persuasion of men made as alike and as unanimous as possible and the discovery by discussion of a common plan which will give scope to differences is discussed in the second and third of these lectures, but the challenge of National Socialism has heightened and intensified it.

I think it may be worth while to say something about the connection which I think undoubtedly exists between these two contrasted theories of government and the two forms which democratic theory has taken.

Modern democracy goes back, as these lectures maintain, to seventeenth century England; but they did not sufficiently emphasize that it had in that period two very different sources: religious experience and physical science. The importance of the religious experience of the seventeenth century has been sufficiently emphasized in the first of these lectures, but I said nothing about the influence of physical science. The acknowledged spiritual ancestor of Bentham as of Karl Marx was Thomas Hobbes. Hobbes invented the Economic Man and the individualism which goes with that conception, and in his conception of human nature he was largely influenced by his desire to model politics and social theory on the methods of the newly invented physical sciences. Professor Halévy has brilliantly shown in his work on the Philosophical Radicals how the same desire to make social theory a science like physics accounts for much in Benthamite psychology. If social theory is to be like physics, its elements must be identical atoms. Hence arise associationist psychology and atomic individualism. The doctrine of human equality for thinkers of this school is a doctrine which conceives men as alike, supposes that their differences are the result of environment, of the different influences to which these identical natures are subjected. As material for the statesman, educator or planner, men are all alike.

Hobbes himself was acute enough to see that if men are really isolated, equipollent units, united only by relations external to their nature, they can only be held together by a power external to them. He had no illusions that such men could make a working democracy. He wanted Hitler and a totalitarian state.

Hobbes' individualism and his conception of human equality had nevertheless a profound effect on democratic theory. By way of the French Encyclopaedists they influenced the English Utilitarians and they produced that radical equalitarianism which is the real opponent of the individualism based on religious experience, and they are the source of most of what I have described in these lectures as the false theory of democracy.

The times we are living in are in many ways behind this 'scientific' individualism. Not only is the theoretical desire to treat society in terms of the physical sciences as strong as it has ever been. There are much more potent practical forces working in the same direction. The tendency of mass production is to smooth out differences between individuals, to have little use for special craftsmanship, to create a civilization of men and women living the same sort of lives, wearing the same sort of clothes, reading the same mass-produced reading matter and enjoying the same amusements. Finally, as the fourth of these lectures pointed out, mass production has evolved a thoroughly non-democratic type of organization, one in which planning and control are centralized in a few hands—where the fundamental distinction in society is between the few who control and plan, and the many who are controlled and planned. The influence of this model of 'scientific' business administration on the new totalitarian government is plain enough. It is equally plain that these superior beings who are going or who think they are going to have the fun of planning will have little use for the eccentricities and personal views or idiosyncracies which make the mass of men less ready to fit into their scheme of planning. Toleration will seem a mischievous absurdity, any independent organization of will a dangerous nuisance, religious minorities a crime against their plans and therefore against the state. They will use all the powers of mass propaganda to back the forces which are already tending to make men more alike. The only religion they will tolerate is devotion to the plan.

There is a remarkable prophetic vision of this outcome of 'scientific' individualism in Nietzsche's account of 'the last man' in the introduction to *Also sprach Zarathustra* and a recent elaboration of the same theme in Mr. Aldous Huxley's *Brave New World*. Hitler's Germany has shown that such visions are not nearly so much only a bad dream as we most of us imagined. It seems also to be showing that religion is the one force which can put up an effective opposition to it.

If democracy and the totalitarian state are at fundamental odds, does this mean that democracy is as incompatible with socialism as it is with Fascism or National Socialism? The economic crisis has apparently made some Socialists think so. Their argument is that when things are going well with capitalism and there is a surplus to be spared, not very much pressure or common regulation is necessary to get from the employing classes such concessions as will content the employed classes; but when the economic machine breaks down, the class war that is always latent in capitalism breaks out undisguised and the basis of democracy disappears. Social justice can then on this view only be secured by revolutionary, that is, non-democratic methods. This is only to say that in our modern industrial system class interests are stronger than common interests and that capitalism so perverts our democratic institutions that nothing fundamentally opposed to the interests of the propertied classes can be carried through constitutionally. Of such statements there can be neither proof nor refutation. Democracy, as I have said in these lectures, depends upon men's sense of their common interests prevailing over their sectional interests. There is no a priori reason why they always should or why at a crisis they should not. That depends on the extent to which the community has a common life, and that it never has completely.

It is true that our class divisions pervert our democracy, it is surely untrue that they pervert it entirely. The writers I am referring to argue that the economic crisis has produced a democratic crisis. Of course it has, but there is no more reason for supposing it to be more impossible to cope with a democratic than with an economic crisis. Democracy, indeed, just because it is alive is always in crisis.

There is a good deal to be said, as was hinted in the last pages of these lectures, for the view that a modern industrial democratic society, with its oligarchically governed industry and its democratic political structure, is a house divided against itself, and that unless we somehow make our industry more democratic, our politics must become more oligarchic. But it depends on ourselves which of these two things shall happen. Some people mean by Socialism nothing else than the application to the government of industry of the democratic principles which have already been applied with such success in politics. So far from such Socialism being inconsistent with democracy, it would be its fulfilment.

But other people mean something very different from that by Socialism, how different is not always realized. They mean the complete carrying on of all economic functions by a centralized state and they combine this practical proposal with the doctrine that only economic matters are of any consequence. Such a Socialism like Bolshevism involves the totalitarian state and is, I think, incompatible with democracy, if these lectures have understood democracy at all aright. This is not because planning and democracy are at all incompatible, but because there is all the difference in the world between planning whose object is to give harmony and consistency to a life which has purposes and movements of its own, or as we said above to give scope for differences, and a planning which purposes to impose an all-comprehensive system to which there is to be no rival. Of course a totalitarian state may have a democratic constitution, but if all centres of organization outside the state are suppressed, isolated individuals have no chance at all against the power of the administration, and a real democracy is impossible.

Marxism is fundamentally incompatible with democracy because its conception of human nature is that of Hobbes. Men who are capable of pursuing only their economic interests are incapable of subordinating these to a common interest. Marxism has never faced the problem of democracy, and that for a curious reason. Benthamism believed in

natural harmony in economics and disharmony in politics
and therefore believed in anarchy in economics and government in politics. Marx thought that economic disharmony
so perverted politics that until that disharmony was removed,
the democratic state was only exploitation by the dominant
class. But he seems to have inverted Benthamism and
thought that if property were publicly owned, and the class
war therefore done away with, the state would wither away
and a natural harmony of interests would take its place.
Democratic government on this view is therefore either
impossible or unnecessary. To believe that any change in
institutions, however far-reaching, is going to remove all
causes of conflict and disharmony among men and render
government unnecessary is so fatuous that, as Aristotle would
have said, no one could maintain it if he were not defending
a theory. This is one of the fatal consequences of the atomic
individualism which has dogged modern democratic theory
from the beginning, and it is only natural that the theory
which has most emphatically denounced religion and exalted
'scientific' materialism, should show so conspicuously the
absurdity of any theories of politics which are its consequence.

September 1935

LECTURE I

WE are at the present time passing through a certain disillusionment about democracy. Before the war it could almost be taken for granted that democracy of some kind or other was the only possible government for a modern civilized country. The surviving nondemocratic elements in a great modern state like Germany were felt to be survivals, alien to the spirit of the age and certain in course of time to disappear. Not that we thought our previous democracies perfect. We found in them a great deal to grumble at. But our grumblings were usually to the effect that our democratic governments were not democratic enough. Socialism for example—that one great school of thought which systematically criticized existing democratic governments, did it on the ground that oligarchically governed industry made democratic politics a sham, made a modern industrial society a house divided against itself; and its remedy was and is the democratization of industry—not less democracy but more.

How different are things now! States like Italy and Spain which never were in any sense real democracies have given up all pretence of being so and glory in having shaken off the cloak they once so proudly assumed. And in the countries like France and England, and, I gather, the United States, where there is no real intention to depart from democracy, there is still a great deal of talk about its failure, or our postwar disillusionment with it. It is again becoming the fashion for superior persons to sneer at democracy. 'As for democracy,' said Alcibiades towards the end of the Peloponnesian war, 'why should we discuss acknowledged madness?' and our young Alcibiades of the present day talk in similar terms.

This contrast between the pre-war and the post-war estimation of democracy is in face of the facts paradoxical. For it was the nondemocractic governments that went to pieces under the strain of the war and the democratic governments which came successfully through and proved their efficiency.

And the new democracy of Germany, the hopeful, alert democracies in the smaller states like Czecho-Slovakia and Esthonia, above all the application in the League of Nations of the principles of democratic government to international relations are far more striking witnesses to the success of democracy than the repudiation by Italy and Spain of a democracy they never possessed are witnesses to its failure. It almost looks as though it was the success and not the failure of democracy which made men disillusioned with it. That, though paradoxical, is, I think, true. Real democracy, when experienced is such a thoroughly satisfactory form of government that men are always trying to extend it and to give it more to do. The tried success of democratic government in Europe and North America in the second half of the nineteenth century was accompanied by the extension of the area of democratic government, and an enormous increase in the functions which men expected a democratic government to perform. What the Webbs have called Industrial Democracy has gone through the same process of development. The English Trade Unions of the early years of the nineteenth century were mostly both small and simple. Their members mostly knew one another and the functions they had to perform were mostly so simple that they were within any one's power. With the development of industry unions had to become national bodies—had to have a membership running into thousands, scattered all over the country—unable to meet together, having to build up amid all sorts of difficulties some sort of representative machinery. And all the time that their area was increasing their work was becoming more complicated and specialized—no longer a work that any one could do in his spare time but work needing expert skill and trained specialized knowledge. And all those new responsibilities which success had brought entailed new machinery and new organization—new adjustments in democracy itself—and men began to feel that for all the size and success and efficiency of this new industrial democracy it had lost something which was the soul and spirit of the simpler, more primitive organizations. It could not at all 'recapture its first fine careless rapture'. That is often the sad result of success. Organization and machinery and efficient administration choke the spirit and disillusionment sets in.

Men feel disillusionment about political democracy, I believe for reasons of the same kind. Just consider the prodigious achievement of democracy in the United States— how it has managed to give orderly and established government to a continent—to an enormous population of all nations and languages—to a society almost inconceivably different from the society known to the Fathers of the Constitution. But this prodigious success has been purchased at a price—the transformation of Democracy into something very different from anything Jefferson and Lincoln ever dreamed of. And as Democracy adjusts itself clumsily and slowly and inadequately to its new tasks, its failures to meet the new opportunities it has itself created are more evident than its success in making them. It is not simply that the new forms Democracy takes on are disappointing to those who knew the old. The position is more serious. The new tasks thrust on successful democracy are really in danger of breaking it down. Expert manipulation of men in the mass, drilled and disciplined parties, and all the other phenomena of modern large-scale democracies are not democracy at all.

Our disappointment with modern political democracy is, I repeat, not the result simply of a comparison between what exists now and what we remember existing in an earlier or simpler time, or what our parents or grandparents have told us. The disillusionment comes from a contrast in the present. We are all of us members of one or more of the innumerable smaller societies which are such a feature of modern social life, particularly of American and English social life. We know there what a thoroughly satisfactory and obvious and altogether to be taken for granted a form of government democracy can be, and we are worried and disappointed because political democracy falls so far short of the experienced ideal.

Is this appeal to the simple, familiar, small society a mistake? Is this feeling of disillusionment unnecessary? Does it arise from our contrasting a nation or world-wide society with what it cannot and never was intended to be like? That the appeal from the state to the small circles of personal relationship is often misleading is plain enough. The history of the doctrine of natural rights—of the conception of human brotherhood, makes that clear. But the persistency of such appeals in the history of politics is witness of how often men know that large organizations and machinery tend to become an end in themselves, and have by such appeals to be reminded of the simple human ends they are intended to serve.

I propose therefore to go back to the beginnings of modern democracy as it was first conceived in the seventeenth century and formulated by men who had had vivid experience of the supereminent satisfactoriness of simple democratic government in the self-governing congregation, and therefore demanded that the state should be organized on the same model. There is this special reason for my going back to the seventeenth century experience when lecturing to an American audience. It is a bold task for an Englishman to talk about Democracy to citizens of the United States. English and American Democracy are in many ways so subtly different: they rest on such different assumptions and have developed in such different ways that it is very hard for a man who is familiar with the one form to talk to those familiar with the other without misunderstanding. If I plunged at once into a discussion of modern conditions you might be tempted to assume that I coming from England necessarily do not know really what Democracy means: and you might be affronted if you seemed, from some of my language, to discover that I thought that it was you as Americans who suffered from that ignorance. But in the seventeenth-century Puritans democrats in America and in England have a common spiritual ancestry and we can begin on common ground examining afresh the rock out of which we both are hewn.

This way of beginning our discussion should have the great advantage of reminding us of the part played in the development of democracy, and still played in its working by the democratically governed religious organizations. On the practical importance of this for the present day I hope to have something to say in a later lecture. But it will help us to have it in mind from the start.

By great good fortune we happen to possess a first hand account—taken down in the shorthand of the period—of a memorable debate on the principles of democratic government and their practical application to England, held between the representatives of the army on the one hand, and the two men who were more than any others really responsible for the government of England, Cromwell and Ireton, on the other. The debate was held at the grand council of officers at Putney, the 25th of October, 1647, to consider a remonstrance from the army called 'The case of the army truly stated, together with the mishaps and dangers which are imminent and some suitable remedies, and humbly proposed by the agents of five regiments of horse to the respective regiments and the whole army.' The officers discussed it with five agents who are named—one of them with the appropriate name of Mr. Wildman, and four soldiers. Some of the most striking remarks are made by one of the latter who is referred to simply as Buffcoat—as might be 'Steel Helmet' or 'The Unknown Soldier'.

The Council of officers were not all in agreement with Cromwell and Ireton. The case for the army is maintained by a Colonel Rainboro, one of the most prominent of the Levellers. For convenience sake therefore I shall refer to those who voice the views of the delegates from the army as the Levellers.

The debate was taken down in shorthand by one William Clarke, who was at that time secretary to the Council of the Army. He was one of those who afterwards followed Monk and was made Secretary at War after the Restoration. His son, Dr. George Clarke, bequeathed his father's papers in 1736 to Worcester College, Oxford, and they were edited by Professor Firth and published by the Camden Society in 1891.

The article in the case for the army round which the debate centres is the demand for manhood suffrage, and in their statements of the case for it its defenders touch the centre of democratic principle. Ireton defends the principle that voting should be based on property and confined to those who have a permanent stake in the country and he argues his case ably and well. But all such arguments based as they are on expediency and experience are swept aside by the passionate vision of the others. 'Really,' said Colonel Rainboro, 'I think the poorest he that is in England hath a life to live as the richest he.' That seems to me the authentic note of democracy. The poorest has his own life *to live*, not to be managed or drilled or used by other people. His life is his and he has to live it. None can divest him of the responsibility. However different men may be in wealth or ability or learning, whether clever or stupid, good or bad, living their life is their concern and their responsibility. That is for those Puritans as for all true democrats the real meaning of human equality. Responsibility for one's own life is something possessed by or enjoined on us all. Our equality in that responsibility is of such preponderating importance that beside it all our other differences, manifest and undeniable as they may be, are neither here nor there. That is not a scientific nor a common-sense doctrine. It is a religious and moral principle. It is the translation into non-theological language of the spiritual priesthood of all believers. Men who could say things like that have gone deep into the heart of things.

But when it comes to drawing the consequences from this simple act of faith, questionings arise. 'And therefore truly I think, Sir, it is clear', goes on Colonel Rainboro, 'that every man that is to live under a government ought first by his own consent to put himself under that government and

I do think that the poorest man in England is not at all bound in a strict sense to that government that he hath not had a voice to put himself under.' And so again, 'Every man born in England, cannot, ought not, neither by the law of God nor the law of nature, to be exempted from the choice of those who are to make laws for him to live under and for aught I know, to lose his life under.'

And so in the same strain, Mr. Wildman:

'I conceive that the undeniable maxim of government is that all government is in the free assent of the people. If so, then upon that account there is no person that is under a just government or hath justly his own, unless he by his free consent be put under that government. This he cannot be unless he be consenting to it and therefore according to this maxim there is never a person in England but ought to have a voice in electing; there are no laws that in this strictness and vigour of justice any man is bound to that are not made by those whom he doth consent to. And therefore I should humbly move that if the question be stated which should soonest bring things to an issue it might return to this: whether any person can justly be bound of law who doth not give his consent that such persons should make laws for him.'

Observe what is beginning to happen. The spiritual principle implied in 'The poorest he hath a life to live in England as well as the richest he' is now translated into the principle that no man has a right to be governed save by his own consent. But as Ireton very truly points out, full consent and government are not really compatible. The principle that we are bound to nothing except we consent to it is really anarchy and nothing else. The Levellers protest that they are not anarchists, but they only manage to maintain that with any plausibility because they are untrue to their principles. What they are content with is not now consent to each and every law but consent to the persons who are to make the law—and even then they are cheating. For the practical measure for which they are contending is that every one should have a right to take part in the electing of legislators. But to say that you have chosen your legislator because you have voted against him is a curious argument, frequently as it is used by those who wish to base government on consent. And yet, unless you accept that absurdity, those insisters on consent must admit that every legislator is invalidly elected who is not elected unanimously. That would of course make government impossible. That is not the worst of it. For when the debate begins Cromwell proposes that they should first see how far those new proposals are compatible with the public engagements into which they have already entered. This provokes a storm of protests from the delegates. The question is—they insist—not what engagements we have entered into but what is right and just—and what is right and just they make abundantly clear is what they think right and just. Buffcoat expresses in unmistakable language their impossibilist temper:

'He could break engagements in case they proved unjust and that it might so appear to his conscience. That whatsoever hopes or obligations I should be bound unto, if afterward God should reveal himself, I would break it speedily, if it were an hundred a day.'

For note lastly that the absolutism of this moral principle is transcribed into an equal absolutism in the application of it and that that is a very different matter. This doctrine of consent is founded on the law of God and the law of nature. It is not something which admits of compromise or need take any account of historical circumstances or existing obligations. The spiritual principle of democracy seems when translated into practice to turn into such impossibilist nonsense that its very defenders for all their absolutist talk, compromise.

These impossibilities Ireton is not slow to point out. 'When I do hear men speak of laying aside all engagements to consider only that wild or vast notion of what in every man's conception is just or unjust, I am afraid that I tremble at the boundless and endless consequences of it.' 'If you will resort only to the law of nature, by the law of nature you have no more right to this land or anything else than I have. I have as much right to take hold of anything that is for my sustenance, to take hold of anything that I desire to my satisfaction as you.' He exposes the inconsistencies of the Levellers by getting them to admit that by 'all men' they do not mean foreigners or even servants. In fact all that admirable common sense and clear logic can say against the Levellers Ireton says.

And yet when he has said all he has to say, you feel that though he may have refuted the Levellers' practical proposals he has never got to grips with what is moving them. He can criticize and does criticize admirably their constitutional suggestions, but he and they are not really moving in the same sphere. They have something to say the spirit of which he does not recognize. In the Levellers and Ireton we have two elements which are visible in all the democratic movements which are to follow them, a mystical conviction of the equality of man which has behind it a living power and fervour, but, if translated literally into practical machinery, is impossibilist and anarchic, and the compromising spirit of the practical man who knows the necessities of government and tries by appeals to common sense and efficiency to get some sense into the idealist. From the give and take of these two elements comes much in later democratic thinking. Perfect democracy becomes an ideal where men are guided solely by the inner voice and yet come to identical conclusions, where government has become consent and coercion has disappeared. But in this present evil world it is recognized to be an impossibility. Government has to be carried on whether people agree or not. Some regard has to be paid to efficiency and some concession made to the glaring actual inequalities between man and man; still more between race and race. Actual governments go some way to meet the idealist but pay more regard to practical exigencies. And the easiest, most disastrous and commonest compromise is to let the idealist go on talking, or let him express himself in declarations of right and high-sounding principles and to see to it in practice that such declarations do no harm and are satisfactorily nullified by what is actually done. For as the principles of the Levellers and of Ireton never meet, they can never really be united.

When, however, we consider what Cromwell has to say we come to something more hopeful. Cromwell shows himself to be both the most religious and the most practical man in the discussion. He has far more sympathy with and understanding of the Levellers than has Ireton. 'I cannot but see that we all speak to the same end and the mistakes are only in the way.' He has not the concern which either they or Ireton have for the machinery of government. 'The Jews had different forms of government and in all those kinds of government they were happy and contented. If you make the best of it, if you should change the government to the best of it, it is but a moral thing. It is but as Paul says, "droess and dung in comparison of Christ".' He remembers all the time that they are discussing plans which are to content not themselves but a nation. 'We are to consider whether according to reason and judgement the spirits and temper of the nation are prepared to receive and go along with it.' But above all he insists from first to last that men who claim to speak in the name of God must be prepared for real discussion, must recognize that they all are fallible, that they can correct one another.

'At such a meeting as this it has been said we should wait upon God and hearken to the voice of God speaking in every one of us. I confess it is an high duty but when anything is spoken as from God I think the rule is: Let the rest judge. It is left to me to judge for my own satisfaction and the satisfaction of others whether it be the Law or not and I do no more.' . . . 'If when we want particular and extraordinary impressions we shall either altogether sit still because we have them not and not follow that light that we have; or shall go against or short of that light that we have upon the imaginary apprehension of such divine impressions and divine discoveries in particular things which are not so divine as to carry their evidence with them to the conviction of those that have the spirit of God within them, I think we shall justly be under a condemnation. Truly we have heard many speaking to us and I cannot but think that in many of those things God hath spoke to us. I cannot but think that in most that have spoke there hath been some things of God made known to us and yet there hath been several contradictions in what hath been spoken. But certainly God is not the author of contradictions.'

Cromwell has as much as the Levellers the fundamental democratic belief in the individual conscience—'This Law and this word speaking within us—which truly is in every man that hath the spirit of God—we are to have a regard to. Our best way is to judge the conformity or disformity of it with the Law written within us which is the law of the spirit of God, the mind of God—the mind of Christ.' He is prepared to listen to and learn from every one—Buffcoat as well as the rest, Lieutenant-General or private. God may have spoken to any one of them. And yet we must distinguish the word of God from our own imaginings, and we are to do that by discussion, by giving weight to the opinions of others and by reason. He also makes a distinction whose importance for democracy I shall discuss later, between knowledge of the will of God which is discovered when men come together in the spirit of God, and knowledge of matters of fact. 'If in those things we do speak or pretend to speak from God, there be mistakes of fact, if there be a mistake in the thing—in the reason of the thing—truly I think it is for me to show both the one and the other if I can.'

Now in this attitude of Cromwell this is perhaps most noteworthy—that while he starts from the same religious democratic basis as the Levellers, believing that God may reveal himself as well through Buffcoat as through the Lieutenant-General, through the poorest him as through the richest him—he has no sympathy—not even as much as Ireton with their doctrine of consent. Ireton and the Levellers are disputing as to whose will or whose consent is to be asked. Democratic machinery is to give expression to will, and the issue between Ireton and the others is whether it is to be the will of men of property or of every one. Cromwell is indifferent to such questions. For him the purpose of such machinery is to find something out, to discover something which is there to be discovered—discovered by hearing what each man's conscience has to say but also by frank and open discussion among men wishing to learn the will of God. What he has learned from his experience of the small democracy of the Christian congregation is the insight into the purposes of life which the common life and discussion of a democratic society can give as nothing else can.

And as we shall see it is this experience and this alone which can save democracy from the impossibilist anarchy which Ireton so abundantly criticized but which rises up time and again to trouble the practical man, just because the Iretons of this world cannot understand or satisfy the real spirit which is behind it.

LECTURE II

WE have seen already from our examination of the discussion in the Clarke Papers that the inspiration of modern democracy came from men's experience of the entirely satisfactory character of democratic government in the Christian congregation—came therefore especially from the Independents, the Anabaptists, and the Quakers—from the men who had both accepted more wholeheartedly than other Protestants the reformation doctrine of the spiritual priesthood of all believers, and made the small independent congregation the unit of government. We have seen at the same time that the moment men sought to apply that experience to political problems difficulties arose.

These difficulties had their origin partly, as I suggested in my last lecture, in differing views as to what was really essential in that experience. The two attitudes represented dramatically in that conversation by Cromwell and the Levellers respectively are typical of two points of view which persist in democracy. The Levellers, we may perhaps say, are all taken up with what this new government feels like. In it every one is made to feel equal and active. The decisions of the small society, when it is working happily, are felt to be the decisions of every member. Their watchword is therefore government by consent. What makes this new form of government so precious is that it is *their* government —that they are all priests. That therefore has to be preserved at all costs. Men must somehow continue to have this feeling that the government is theirs and that they give their consent to it.

Cromwell, a man both of deeper spiritual insight and of far greater practical ability and experience, is concerned with the conditions under which alone this happy experience is realized. Consent is for him a result and not a condition. He conceives its conditions to be that all concerned are seeking to express not their own will but the will of God. That is something to the discovery of which all may contribute, but only in so far as they are ready to discuss freely and unreservedly with others; and to use what knowledge and experience of the situation they have.

But the difficulties of the application of the experience of the simple democratic society to politics arose not only from those different interpretations. They were the inevitable result of the differences of the situation to which this newly-won experience was now applied.

The most obvious and the most persistent and puzzling of these differences is the difference in scale. It is not the only difference which matters. The difference in the purpose and nature of a political society from other forms of association is, as we shall see, another difference of great importance. But so long as we do not forget that there is this other fundamental difference to be considered, we can begin by considering by itself this difference in scale and its far-reaching effects.

Churches are voluntary organizations, and the Independents and Anabaptists could make the single congregation the unit of government if they wished; and they could also make each unit within limits self-contained. But the size of the unit of political government is not dictated by the ideal conditions of governing but by the nature of the work to be done, by all kinds of geographical, economic, and historical circumstances. As civilization has developed, communications become easier and commerce more important, the areas needing common governmental control have become steadily larger. The discrepancy between the area of government dictated by the capacity for good governing and the area dictated by the need for government is one of the most baffling disharmonies of politics, and is with us all. It appears in its most formidable and insurmountable form when any attempt is made to transfer the experience of the small self-enclosed democratic society to political government.

Something very wonderful can, as Cromwell saw, come

out of the close association of a small body of men—small enough for it to be possible for them all to know one another, and for real discussion—a constructive effort of collective thinking—to be possible. But how tiny has such a society to be? How many people can meet for discussion in such a way that anything real can come out of the discussion? It depends, I think, on how well they know one another. The ideal number varies, but it is not large.

'The best number of members for a University's principal governing board,' wrote President Eliot,[1] 'is seven: because that number of men can sit round a small table, talk with each other informally without waste of words or any display or pretence, provide an adequate diversity of points of view and modes of dealing with the subject in hand, and yet be prompt and efficient in the despatch of business. In a board of seven the different professions and callings can be sufficiently represented.'

That is of course an extreme view. There can, as the experience of the Christian congregation proved, be a meeting of a much larger number of people who, if they know one another, can really come to a creative agreement and produce that mysterious thing called 'the sense of the meeting', even when only few take part in the discussion. But the limits of a meeting of that sort are soon reached. How many movements there are in democratic societies which are started by a few people who understand one another, pool their difficulties and suggestions, and then build up a movement by the creative energy which comes from discussions of that kind, who then find that the size of the movement has made impossible the kind of government which built it up! There are some societies which never recover from their success.

It is a commonplace of political theory that direct democracy became impossible when the size of the community outgrew the limits of a single public meeting. But long before that limit is reached most members of the community

[1] *University Administration*, C. W. Eliot.

have ceased to take any part in the discussion or to contribute anything to the meeting. No one can really do business at a big meeting. Men can say Yes or No to cut-and-dried proposals, or compelling and spellbinding speeches may turn votes, but the real discussion and largely the real government is in the hands of the committee who prepare the business.

The real point is that when a society has grown beyond the limits of a public meeting, then even the pretence of direct government has to be given up, and something has to be done about it. And that the limit of direct democracy was felt to be determined by the limit in the size of the public meeting, and not by the much earlier limit of the effective discussion, has been of sinister importance in the theory of democracy. It has suggested that what matters is not that the people should rule, but that they should think they rule; and it has given undue emphasis to the element of consent over the element of discussion.

But the practical man will be listening to all this with growing impatience. How far away all such discussions seem from the actual necessities of government even in the seventeenth century! The population of the nation state even then ran into millions. What relation could there possibly be between the government of millions, scattered over a wide area, with little knowledge of one another, and the government of a congregation? Ought we not to say frankly that in these circumstances government by the people is an obvious impossibility? Government, even if it be government by means of discussion, can only be carried on by a few, and that is surely the end of it.

We are accustomed to say that this problem was solved by representative government. That representative government was adopted because of this difficulty of size is true enough. 'In Massachusetts', says Bourgeaud,[1] 'the fact that the electors were scattered over a wide tract of country led to the adoption of the representative system. After 1634 the

[1] Bourgeaud, *Rise of Modern Democracy*, p. 153.

General Assembly of Boston became practically an assembly of delegates.' It was the great invention of representative government (so the accepted theory of government runs) which enabled modern democracy to pass the narrow limits within which Greek democracy was confined—limits defined by Aristotle as the range of an orator's voice.

But the different attitudes to democracy which I have symbolized by the Levellers and Cromwell have expressed themselves in very different attitudes to representative government. Let us examine each of these separately, remembering that the two attitudes are in fact always both operative—that they represent two aspects, both of which are necessary to democracy. We shall be examining separately what does not exist separately. The facts will always be better than the description of either tendency would suggest. For, as we shall see, either of these attitudes, though it may be exalted by its adherents as the essential of democracy, leads, if not corrected by the other, to a denial of democracy.

With that warning in our minds, let us examine first the attitude of the Levellers and their followers to representative government. The Levellers themselves had no intention of setting up a sovereign representative assembly. Their legislature was to be limited by a fundamental law, withdrawing certain fundamental matters from the control of their representatives. Our friend Mr. Wildman[1] writes, 'I believe that the freedomes of this nation will never be secure, until the extent of the power and trust of the people's representatives and the people's reservations to themselves be clearly defined.' Democratic theory, following the lead of the Levellers, has never been entirely happy about the representative. He is a necessary evil, to be done without if possible. Think of the disputes which have raged round the difference between representative and delegate—round the proper relation of a representative to his constituents—of Walt Whitman's protest against 'the never-ending audacity of elected persons'—of the very different answers given to

[1] *Truth's Triumph*, quoted Bourgeaud, p. 89.

the puzzling question, 'What does a representative represent?' 'If any one should inquire', says the Agreement of
the People,[1] 'why we should desire to join in an agreement
with the people to declare these to be our native rights, and
not rather to petition to the Parliament for them: the reason
is evident. No Act of Parliament is or can be unalterable
and so cannot be sufficient security to save you or us harm-
lesse, from what another Parliament may determine, if it
should be corrupted.' Rousseau confirmed this attitude in
his statement that the people of England are free only at a
general election, and that then they enslave themselves.
From Rousseau till the present day there is a continuous
tradition in democratic theory which had denounced representative government as essentially undemocratic—or at least
as a makeshift to be controlled and limited as much as possible,
and democratic practice in Switzerland and America, if not
in England, has made experiment after experiment to embody
this tradition in practice.

Let us accept the position of the Levellers that the consent
to government and to acts of government by each and every
member of the community is the one thing needful to democracy—that therefore government by the public meeting,
where such is possible, is its ideal form—and with that in
mind let us think again of Aristotle's limit of democracy—
the range of an orator's voice; and remember that there are
now other ways than representative government of setting
back these limits. Thanks to broadcasting, the whole world
might become in some sense a public meeting. Certainly all
the world could listen to a debate. You in America have just
had the experience of a continent listening to a debate, and
saying Yes and No on a fixed day to the proposals put before
them. And long before radio was invented, skilful reporting
and a cheap Press had done something of the same thing.
They had transformed the representative assembly into
the platform of a public meeting. On it men talked only
partially to one another and increasingly to the invisible

[1] Bourgeaud, p. 89.

public behind. As these representatives ceased to be in fact a sovereign assembly, whatever they remained in name, and became a platform of the public meeting of the nation, it became more important to reach and influence the listeners in the body of the hall than to convince the other side on the platform, and in time the uniqueness and importance of the platform began to diminish. It was felt that so long as the listeners in the body of the hall were reached, it did not very much matter on what particular platform the speaker was standing. Politicians began to tour the country, speaking to mass meetings but always at the same time speaking to the general public beyond—as any statesman important enough to be fully reported always does. Public opinion, instead of being something expressing itself only at authorized times and only in a choice of representatives, became something always there—always being influenced and influencing—an invisible public meeting of the whole country in perpetual session, with the Press a new and indispensable organ of government. Those who experienced the General Strike in England in 1926, with the Press suddenly for all practical purposes put out of action, realized how dependent modern government is on reaching the public all the time. Addressing this invisible but potent audience needed a new technique, and the organization of political propaganda became the absorbing business of political parties, and the two indispensable instruments of the process—the Press and campaign expenses—became more and more important in politics.

The logical conclusion of the whole process is that if we can make the whole country one public meeting, we can make it govern and say Yes or No at the end of the discussion, and so we are to regard the referendum as the logical outcome of democracy. We may even go further and let there be demands from the body of the hall that something else should be discussed—instead of letting the preparation of the agenda be confined entirely to the platform, and then we shall add to the referendum the initiative.

An inevitable result of this process is what is called the decline of representative assemblies. It is obvious enough that thanks to modern publicity methods the United States during a Presidential election becomes one vast public meeting. Indeed, without these publicity methods and party conventions and all the rest of it, the people of the United States could not possibly choose between two candidates as they do. But what a curious public meeting it is—dependent for its existence as a public meeting on the operation of that mysterious and elusive medium we call publicity. What happens in a superlative degree at a Presidential election (and has therefore made the Electoral College practically non-existent) is happening to some extent all the time in modern democracy. Hence the extraordinary fate of the Electoral College is only an extreme example of the fate that is threatening to overcome all representative assemblies —a fate which, *if* the end of democracy is government by public meeting, is inevitable and right. *If* their work is just to make the people listen, they do not, any of them, do that work very well. Are we therefore to say of representative assemblies that they had their place before the development of a cheap Press and other means of addressing a nation-wide public had made possible this new way of widening the range of democratic government; but that now that we have discovered how to make the country into one great public meeting, they are not wanted and their decay is not to be mourned?

In spite however of the help which democracy now gets from modern science, this process of widening the area of democratic government is disillusioning. Modern democracy does not feel like the simple town meeting or the congregation. What has gone wrong?

Of course one thing which is obviously wrong in this new and magical public meeting is that the means of transmission of sound are unsatisfactory. They do not transmit anything like all that is said on the platform: and a great deal of what they do transmit, they transmit wrong. That is the problem of the Press. What we have done is to let into this public meeting a private transmitting medium, which really controls what the public hears. In England at least that transmitting medium is coming under the control of fewer and fewer people. The remedy would appear to be that the Press be made public. That has practical difficulties. But even apart from these, people who believe in that cure for our problem had better study the files of the *British Gazette*, which did perform the function suggested during the British General Strike in 1926. No doubt, however, there are various devices by which private interests could be kept from exploiting the machinery of the public meeting.

But before we think of considering any proposals towards that end, let us ask ourselves whether we really want to make government like an immense public meeting. Does any sane man think that a desirable end to bring about? What did anyone ever *do* at a public meeting except produce enthusiasm? Look at the practice of largish democratic societies, and observe that when they hold their congresses they may have public meetings for propaganda purposes, but they never attempt more than the most formal business at them. Government by public meeting is an impossibility, as anyone must recognize who will think what a public meeting can actually do, or has seen a public meeting unexpectedly asked to do something. When we think of modern democracy as Greek democracy enlarged by modern inventions, we should remember that the Greeks did not think that a state which was, as we say, governed by a public meeting was necessarily a democracy. For them the test question was—what was the constitution of the body which arranged the agenda for and managed the public meeting? Only if that were elected by lot (were what President Lowell calls a sample democracy) did they call the state a democracy. Otherwise it was an oligarchy, governed by the few who arranged the business, settled what questions were to be asked, and arranged the discussion. It is not merely that a public meeting can only say Yes or No to questions put to

it, or that public meetings whether of visible or invisible
audiences are notoriously susceptible to mass suggestion,
but that whether they say Yes or No depends enormously
on how the questions are put, and on what sort of discussion
there is.

Further it is worth noting that most of (though not all)
the effective criticisms of democracy are criticisms of what
happens at the public meeting, visible and invisible. The
anti-democrat calls democracy government by a mob. But
a collection of people is not in itself a mob, and it is not made
a mob because its members are common or ordinary or
stupid people, but because and in so far as they are under
the influence of mass suggestion. The individual members of
the most howling mob would be found to be sensible decent
people in their own cricle when dealing with familiar problems which they have to face as a matter of business. The
anti-democrat who contemplates certain aspects of the public
meeting may well say of democracy, if it is government by
public meeting, that it is government by mass suggestion;
that its implication is that people govern best by getting
themselves into a state of mind in which they would never
dream of getting to solve their own comparatively simple
problems. No one supposes that in ordinary life the responses
of people under mass suggestion are of any serious value
whatever. No one in his senses, if he had to solve an ordinary
scientific or practical problem, would put himself under mass
suggestion. The anti-democrat contemplating much that
goes on at a general election may well ask—what are we to
think of a form of government in which people deliberately
make themselves drunk, or allow themselves to be made
drunk, before they decide the most important questions of
government? For there is no very essential difference in the
effects on the judgement of mass suggestion and of alcohol.
And the cynically-minded might say that it was not an
accident that in the early days of democracy election days
were great days of drunkenness: that if the liquor has now
largely disappeared, that is partly because the required result

can be produced without it; the effectiveness of mass suggestion has so much increased.

These are surely elementary considerations—so elementary are they, and so unanswerable are some of these anti-democratic criticisms, that their neglect in much modern democracy requires explanation. Men surely could not so ignore simple facts if they were not under the influence of some compelling theory.

The theory which forces men to acquiesce in these evils is the theory of the Levellers that the essence of democracy is government by the consent of all the governed—that that result is more important than are the means by which it is attained. That is, as we saw, an impossible ideal, in any real sense of the word 'consent'. But if it is accepted as an ideal, democrats will hold that the measure of democracy is the amount of consenting by everybody that there is. The Levellers could only conceive of one general consent to the fundamental form of government. We can do better than that—we can make the necessity of consent more frequent and can insist that our governors should come for our consent for everything they do.

But when we set our minds to bring this about, certain puzzling questions and disquieting facts arise. Is democracy a means of bringing about that the people shall consent to what the government proposes to do, or that the government shall do what the people want? The two things are very different, and yet if all we want is to produce consent, it can be got in either way. If we choose the second alternative as being obviously the more democratic, we shall have to ask ourselves whether the people do want anything definitely and unanimously enough for there to be any sense in the second alternative. Shall we not have to say that no constructive proposals can possibly come from the people as a whole? Constructive and definite proposals come from individuals or tiny groups of individuals. In any real sense of the words 'wish' or 'want' the people do not wish or want anything. Their approval or disapproval, their liking or disliking of what individuals or small groups of individuals put before them will be real enough—but that is another matter. Strictly speaking, phrases such as 'the will of the people' or 'the voice of the people' are mere mythology. The great mass of the people can only consent to what government or some other organized group of people proposes to do. If the formulation of proposals or the choice of alternative candidates is not done by a responsible government organization, it will have to be done by an irresponsible organization—as a study of political parties has long made evident. The only result of insisting on the pretence that the people shall do it is to transfer the work of formulating proposals from the responsible to the irresponsible organization.

We are thus thrown back on the first alternative—that the people shall consent to what the government want to do. But then we have to ask whether that means that the government shall spend their time in trying to discover to what proposals the people shall give, as it were, spontaneous consent, or in making up their minds what ought to be done or what the occasion requires, and then trying to get consent to it. And *if* the mark of democracy is consent as nearly as possible unanimous, the second way of getting consent is much the simpler. Mass propaganda and mass persuasion will then be the real instrument of democratic government.

There is worse to follow. For if you are really out for unanimity, experience from Puritan Massachusetts to Fascist Italy has shown that a dissentient minority will be 'learnt to be unanimous'. There must then be a monopoly of the means of mass persuasion: minorities and opposition parties must be suppressed, and dissentients in various ways discouraged. Then we shall find (as Plato observed long ago) that the attempt to get complete democracy ends in tyranny. There are traces of the beginnings of Caesarism in all modern democracies, and we shall have to admit that there is more than elsewhere unanimity, and therefore on this theory real democracy, in Fascist Italy and Bolshevist Russia—in the countries which achieve unanimity by the simple means of a monopoly of mass propaganda and a forcible suppression of dissentients.

This paradoxical conclusion suggests that there is something wrong with the argument, that democracy is not just government by consent, and that representative government is more than a mere means of widening the area of the public meeting. Let us therefore look for a little at the alternative theory.

LECTURE III

WE have been examining the results in large-scale government of that interpretation of democracy which regards its essence as the assent of the governed to the acts of government, and have seen that if it is left to itself it produces Caesarism. The attempt to regard representative government as merely a means of producing a public meeting on a nation-wide scale has proved its mistakenness in the paradox to which it led. We are now to see if the other attitude towards democracy—that which counts discussion as more important than consent—will give us a better understanding of representative government.

There is one great difference, besides the difference of scale, between modern representative government and Greek democracy, which we have not yet noticed. Modern representative government implies an organized and official opposition. It does not only tolerate difference and criticism. It implies and demands it. It is the sense of this which is behind the oft-quoted statement that the English people dislike coalitions: or behind the curious complaints which Parliamentary governments with strong majorities often make, that the opposition is not strong or effective enough. How curiously paradoxical is this attitude on the face of it! Ministers who have spent much energy and breath on public platforms denouncing the foolishness and perversity of their opponents, in insinuating that no man in his senses could possibly vote for such misguided people, would be very much disturbed if they were universally taken at their word. It is, I think, clear that so far from unanimous consent being the ideal of representative democracy, representative democracy would not know what to do with such a consummation. Most of us dislike criticism, and in the heat of the moment all opposition tends to be regarded as factious, and yet the modern democratic statesman, for all the hard words he may fling at the opposition and the character of their criticism, knows that he cannot get on without it. We often discuss whether representative government flourishes best with two parties or with more. But no one with the least understanding of its nature would think that it could get on with one party. I was discussing the other day with a Chinese student how the present government of China could become really democratic, and we both took for granted that that was identical with the question how could an authorized and effective opposition be created. The Bolshevik maxim, adopted by Kuo-Min-Tang, 'no opposition party and no opposition within the party', is the antithesis of democracy.

All this is of course a commonplace, but I am not sure that we always realize how much of the essence of democracy is contained in this insistence on a tolerated and official opposition. It implies that the business of representative government is to make articulate and get expressed different not consentaneous points of view—that democratic equality is not an equality of sameness but of difference—that we want every one to have political rights, not because and in so far as they agree with other people, but because and in so far as they have each their peculiar contribution to make. But that after all is the principle behind Colonel Rainboro's 'the poorest he that is in England hath a life to live as the richest he'. Of course if we concentrate on such difference and uniqueness we shall get the kind of anarchy and antinomianism which made the early Quakers such a trouble to Cromwell and which disturbed the beginnings of Rhode Island. But democracy is based on the assumption that men can agree on common action which yet leaves each to live his own life—that if we really respect one another's personality we can find a common framework or system of rights within which the free moral life of the individual is possible.

How that can best be attained can be discovered by discussion, in which the one-sidedness of particular views can be eliminated and a principle of common action discovered which each can feel does justice to what was vital in his own contention. This is Cromwell's position—toleration and recognition of differences, based on the belief that God may speak through any member of the community, combined with insistence that individual views shall submit to the criticism of open discussion.

Now surely, if we reflect upon it, what matters most in the tiny democratic societies which we feel to be thoroughly satisfactory forms of government is what comes out of the free give and take of discussion. When men who are serving a common purpose meet to pool their experience, to air their difficulties and even their discontents, there comes about a real process of collective thinking. The narrowness and one-sidedness of each person's point of view are corrected, and something emerges which each can recognize as embodying the truth of what he stood for, and yet (or rather therefore) is seen to serve the purpose of the society better than what anyone conceived for himself. That is of course an ideal. Such perfect agreement is not often reached. But it is an ideal which is always to some extent realized when there is open and frank discussion. And any one with experience of the effectiveness of discussion in a small democratic society must recognize how valuable is the contribution of those who are not easily convinced but can stand up resolutely for their own point of view. Where discussion of that kind prevails, we recognize that democracy is not a makeshift or a compromise or a means of keeping people quiet by the production of a sham unanimity, or a process of counting heads to save the trouble of breaking them, but the ideal form of government.

Observe further that the moment we take discussion seriously, we are committed to the view that we are concerned not primarily to obtain or register consent, but to find something out. What it is that democratic discussion is trying to find out we shall discuss later. The root of the matter is that if the discussion is at all successful, we discover something from it which could have been discovered in no other way. I am only concerned now to note and insist on this fact, and to note its likeness to the discovery of truth in other spheres. Modern science is a great realm of co-operative thinking where discoveries are made originally by the work of isolated individuals, but where they are tested and enlarged by criticism and discussion. Every scientific discoverer knows that what he most wants to know is not what can be said for, but what can be said against his theory. What he most wants is an opposition. The example of scientific co-operative thinking may remind us that democratic discussion is entirely compatible with leadership and with any amount of difference in the weight of the contributions made by different members. Democracy assumes that each member of the community has something to contribute if it can be got out of him. It does not for a moment assume that what each member contributes is of equal value.

Now if, with all this in mind, we approach the problem created by the large scale of political democracy, we shall say that what matters is not that the final decision of government should be assented to by every one, but that every one should have somehow made his contribution to that decision. There cannot possibly be one enormous discussion, but there may be smaller areas of discussion, and the results of these may be conveyed by the representative to a further discussion, and so on. If we examine the means by which non-political democratic societies which have grown beyond the area of a discussion group try to keep the society democratic, we find the process of representation at its best. A comparatively large voluntary society, with a membership running into thousands, can keep the real spirit of democracy provided that its primary units of discussion—its branches or lodges— are vigorous and alive. If that condition is fulfilled, representatives of branches may then meet by districts for common discussion, and representatives of district meetings may meet for discussion at the General Council of the whole society. The government of that most democratic of all religious societies—the Society of Friends—is an excellent example of this kind of representative democracy. Presbyterian govern-

ment is another example. There the original unit of democratic church government—the congregation—is represented
at the Presbyteries as Presbyteries are represented at Synod
and General Assembly. What matters is that at all stages
there should be effective discussion.

Political representative democracy of course falls far short
of such an ideal. For one thing, its primary units, the constituencies, are far too large for effective discussion; and
not nearly enough attention has been paid to the limits of
effective discussion in the organization of representative
assemblies. But in spite of these obvious defects modern
representative government when it is successful does make
possible an immense deal of real and effective discussion.
How different a view do we get of the processes of modern
democracy whenever we come within range of discussion
with a tolerated and organized opposition. One gets an
impression sometimes as though there were always two
processes going on in politics—on the one hand a process
of producing collective enthusiasm at party meetings (or the
subtler and perhaps more poisonous, if calmer, process of
producing political self-complacency when men of the same
political persuasion deplore in common the folly and knavery
of their political opponents), and on the other hand a great
process of discussion between men who do not agree but do
discuss their disagreements. The final stage of that is of
course the well-regulated give and take discussion which
takes place in an effective legislative assembly. Complaints
are often made nowadays of the unreal character which
strict party voting has given to Parliamentary discussion. But
men with inside experience of politics will usually tell you
that the effect of an able and critical opposition is seen least
in the division lists. But besides the final and formal stage
in the legislative assembly there is in modern democracy an
immense deal of real informal discussion. Though, therefore,
processes of producing collective enthusiasm are depressingly
in evidence, discussion always educative and sometimes
illuminating is there as well. In spite of all the mass propa-

ganda and collective enthusiasm which characterize a General or a Presidential Election, these recurrent crises produce a great amount of political education. It looks as if the application of broadcasting to politics will, if it is regulated so as to ensure fair discussion, make very remarkably for political education as against production of mass consciousness.

Some of the most creative political proposals in modern democracy originate, not with government nor with the permanent Civil Service, but with public-minded voluntary groups, who have a public concern for this or that problem and who have together thought out a remedy for it. We make a great mistake if in considering political democracy we think only of individuals on the one hand and of the political organizations on the other, and neglect the enormous importance in the production of a real public opinion of the innumerable voluntary associations of all kinds which exist in modern democratic society. One aspect of that view of democracy of which Roger Williams and Oliver Cromwell are the first representatives is the independence of church and state. The corollary of that is Lord Acton's doctrine that liberty is possible only in a society where there are centres of organization other than the political. Nothing so much makes possible a public opinion which is real because it is based on free and frank discussion as the existence of independent voluntary organizations with public purposes.

But this comparatively rosy picture has another side, and it is time that we looked at it. We have seen the evils resultant on considering that democracy ought to be government by as much consent as can be got: but there are other evils resultant on considering democracy as nothing but government by discussion groups. The discussion group which is to make effective decisions must be small, but small societies easily breed a spirit of their own—a sort of group-consciousness which resents criticism from outside and easily becomes exclusive. This is true even in the non-political democratic societies where, for reasons which we shall discuss later,

devotion to the purpose of the society can be more taken
for granted than it can in politics. President Eliot supplemented his statement of the ideal discussion group for the
government of a university by insisting that such a group
needs to have its decisions reviewed by a wider body repre-
senting more directly all concerned in the University. The
natural exclusiveness of a small group will always tend to
produce 'the never-ending audacity of elected persons'.

If this is true of such societies, imagine what democratic
political government would be like if all its representative
assemblies were not made in some way continually subject
to public opinion and the light of publicity—what openings
there would be for wire-pulling and log-rolling. We do
not indeed need to imagine such a hypothetical case. Can
we not see in actual fact how continually there is a conflict
between group interests and the community as a whole;
how even organizations which exist to promote ends service-
able to the community—churches, for example, may easily
press their special point of view or their special interests as
organizations against the interests of the community as a
whole? The most effective and creative discussion comes
from a group who know each other intimately and can
therefore discuss informally and with ease. An immense
amount of the most useful work in society is done by such
informal circles. But their informal and unseen power, if
perverted, can be terribly insidious. The political influence
of all these societies which exist for the furtherance of this
or that public cause is not without its dangers, good on the
whole as it is. Religious and semi-religious organizations
have a tendency to identify the Kingdom of God with the
progress of their own particular creed or nostrum, and when
they do that they have a way of doing things in the name of
that sacred cause which no ordinary decent person would do
in the pursuit of his own interests.

These are evils incident to all representative democracy.
But political representative democracy has special dangers of
its own. Political government implies power backed by

compulsion, and there are always in a community individuals and interests eager to capture that power and pervert it to private ends. Remove a representative assembly from the constant watchfulness of public opinion, and it will be remarkable if it escapes corruption. It has been said that one of the advantages of Parliamentary over Presidential government is that because in Parliamentary government debates in Parliament may mean the fall of the government they are followed with more interest by the general public and therefore go on under the constant criticism of public opinion more than do the debates of a representative assembly under Presidential government. Whether that is true or not, I am not concerned to discuss, though I think it is. I wish only to note the assumption that underlies the argument—that it is of paramount importance to the health of a representative assembly that public opinion should be focussed on its doings. We must have real discussion, and we must insist therefore that our representative assemblies shall be so constituted, and have such a procedure, that real discussion is possible in them. But that discussion is to take place, if possible, with the invisible public listening; and the function of a general election is not simply to choose representatives but to express the approval or disapproval of the general public on the doings of the representative assembly. Of course, in a healthy and educated democracy, discussion, as we have already said, will not be confined to the discussions of the representative assembly. The discussion of the assembly will define issues. Profitable discussion in even the smallest group, as we all know, needs a chairman to define issues and focus attention on the points where discussion will be profitable. In a healthy democracy the discussions of the representative assembly will as it were act as chairman for the multifarious informal discussion of the nation as a whole, and the measure of the successful working of democracy is the extent to which the voting of the ordinary man and woman has been informed by this widely diffused public discussion.

But when all this is said, the importance of voting, of taking part in the decision, saying Yes or No on the broad issues formulated by the representative assembly, remains. However strongly we may hold that discussion rather than consent is the thing most worth having in democracy, we know this to be the case. It was no answer to the advocates of female suffrage that women could take part in political discussion as well as men, and therefore could without the vote already make their contribution. It was demanded that their discussion and influence should have behind it the power of the vote, and that that was a real demand was universally recognized. The doctrine of 'virtual representation' has always been seen to be as a subterfuge.

When then does the process of counting heads add to government by discussion?

Before we try to answer that question, let us stop for a moment and consider where the argument has taken us. We saw in the last lecture that government by consent, if taken strictly, is and must be an illusion: that it is an entire mistake to suppose that there exists at any moment a ready-made will of the people. We have only to examine the working of a small democratic society to see that. The process of discovering what may be called the will of the society is a process of making it, and to that process discussion is essential. We saw also that if the advocates of consent take a lower ground, and agree that all constructive and definite proposals must come from the few who form the government, but maintain that it is the essence of democratic government that those proposals should be submitted to the people for their assent or dissent; that under these circumstances—without the check which only an organized opposition can afford—consent can be manufactured. Government by plebiscite is successful Caesarism. We have seen further that the purpose of representative government is to maintain and preserve different points of view, in order to make effective discussion possible: that it is democratic in so far as it recognized that every one, just because they have their own life to lead, has

something special and distinctive to contribute, but that it
gets over the impossibility of large-scale discussion by
dividing the unifying of differences through discussion into
several stages. But we recognized that this belief that every
one has something to contribute does not mean that what
every one has to say is of equal value. It assumes that if the
discussion is good enough the proper value of each contribution will be brought out in the discussion. We have agreed
lastly that unless this discussion is open to the breath of
public criticism, the discussion group may pursue selfish
aims or be corrupted.

Now all this process of discussion is, however complicated
and arranged for, a natural process—grounded in the facts
of human nature. In comparison, is there not something
curiously artificial about voting? The purpose of discussion
is to achieve a real unity of purpose out of differences. The
principle of voting says that all are to count alike. Democratic instinct has always rejected, and surely rightly, schemes
to differentiate voters—to give men more votes because they
are richer or better educated than other people. There have
of course been many attempts in modern democratic governments to weight votes; but such proposals or enactments
have ordinarily, and I think justly, been held to be undemocratic. The democratic opponents of such devices
would say that they do not deny the difference between
men's political capacities, but would maintain that wealth or
wisdom or leadership will have their natural effect in the
discussion that precedes the voting, and no doubt therefore
on the voting. But in the voting itself, they would maintain,
each is to count for one and no one for more than one.
Votes are not really all of equal value, but they are all to be
counted as equal. That is the real paradox of democratic
government which continually provokes the scorn of non-
democratic critics, and yet it is, I think, a paradox which the
democrat must somehow defend at all costs.

In the second place, the principle of voting rests on the
convention that what commands the assent of the majority

of voters (either a bare majority or some specified majority of voters) shall be deemed to be the decision of the whole. That again is something conventional which needs justification.

We shall best approach this question, I believe, by going back to our simple small democracy. There what strikes us is that in a sufficiently small democratic group which is working well there is often very little voting. The part elsewhere played by voting is there played by what is called the sense of the meeting. Let us ask ourselves what that part is. You may have in the small religious democracy a meeting in which only a few take part in discussion. There can never be many taking part in a profitable discussion. But when things are going right, that discussion is dominated and controlled by the sense of the meeting. What that means for the purposes of democracy is this. The creativeness of discussion assumes a common purpose animating those who take part in it. They are trying to find something out. They are asking what the purpose of their community requires. And though a society may have purposes which can be judged by an external standard, the purpose of a religious community—or for that matter the purpose of an educational community like a college—is only realizable and comprehensible in terms of common life, common activity, common experience, something (however described) which can only be known from inside. These purposes have of course other aspects which can be known and studied from without and which may be therefore matters for experts. But though such experts speak with the tongues of men and of angels, though they have the gift of prophecy and understand all mysteries and all knowledge . . . and have not love—are not subdued and dominated by the purpose of the community as it is realized in its common life and activities—then, as the apostle says, they are nothing. The moment that those discussing begin to play for their own hands, or try to enforce their own personal will, the purpose of the discussion is lost. The sense of the meeting, when it is effective, ensures that the discussion shall serve and be controlled by the common purpose. To that end every one contributes, and the contribution of all is necessary.

In such a meeting voting is usually unnecessary, but it is wanted when anything goes wrong. If a too dominant chairman or a dominant group try to force their will on the meeting, the only remedy is to vote, and the equality of the voting is based on the fact of the equality described above—the equality of sharing in the common purpose of the society.

Of course voting is also used much more often for purposes of convenience. When there is not time or possibility of resolving differences, when the one creative proposal which would unite all differences has not been discovered, and we have to choose between more or less satisfactory proposals, the necessity for acting in this world will not wait on our finding the entirely satisfactory solution which would resolve all our differences. We have to act, and to act promptly with what light we have, and action is decisive. Therefore we have to have a rough-and-ready way of deciding between such alternatives as have presented themselves. Equal counting of heads and agreement to abide by the majority vote are rough-and-ready means of getting a second best decision.

There is a special kind of majority rule, very important in politics, which is worth noting and helps to elucidate the point I am making, and that is the rule of a majority party. There may be differences within a community which cannot be resolved by discussion but only by action. The necessary maintaining and organizing of opposition may and often does set up differences too sharply held to be reconciled. 'It is the business of an opposition to oppose,' as the maxim says. But these differences may be and often are reconciled by giving each party a turn to carry out its policy. Then it is found that for all the fire with which the opposition opposed each and every clause of a government's bill, they do not reverse it all when they get the chance. Good representative government, as we all recognize, needs not only a strong opposition. It needs also that the opposition should

be an alternative government. In the alternation in power
of political parties there is often worked out in practical
dialectic what discussion could not discover.

The theory behind the whole procedure is that we are
trying by expression and discussion of different standpoints
to find out what the purpose of the community requires, and
that of *that* the ordinary member of the community is as
good a judge as anyone else, provided (and the proviso is,
as we shall see, of enormous importance)—provided that he
understands what the proposals between which he is judging
really amount to. Rousseau is often supposed to have said
that the general will is always right. He did not. He said it
was always honest. What he was insisting on was the power
of the ordinary man to judge of fair play, of honesty, of
conformance with the spirit of the community. It is this
sense which the ordinary man can contribute and to which
the expert, absorbed as he naturally is in his own solution
and in his special contribution, often fails to contribute.

It seems a far cry from a small religious meeting to the
government of a country. Can we really maintain that there
is anything in national politics in the least corresponding to
the sense of the meeting, and that voting on national issues
or at general elections is in any sense a rough-and-ready way
of taking the sense of the meeting?

This question cannot really be answered properly till we
have tried to answer the question which, as Plato would say,
has kept raising its head all through these last two lectures—
what is the difference between the purpose and nature of a
political society or a state, and of such non-political societies
as we have mostly been discussing? We deliberately post-
poned that question in order to concentrate on the problems
created for all democratic societies alike by the size of the
community. We may perhaps agree that in large scale
non-political democratic societies the problems created by
largeness of scale can be more or less satisfactorily solved if
we go about it in the right way: if we get discussion and
voting into their proper relations and contrive to keep what

people call 'the spirit of the movement' alive and dominating. Such a consummation entails a vast deal of dull sitting in committees and attention to routine and all the rest of it, but it is possible and well worth while.

But political democracy seems incredibly far from any such ideal. It seems obsessed by all kinds of evils of its own. So pervasive and ineradicable do these evils seem to be that it may appear just absurd to attempt to apply a term like 'the sense of the meeting' to political democracy.

There obviously is something peculiar about the state which we shall try to clear up in the next lecture, but we may note now one or two empirical facts which suggest that our procedure of trying to understand political democracy by the study of non-political democratic societies is not beside the mark.

It is a commonplace that successful political democracy on a large scale implies something we call nationality. There has been endless discussion on what constitutes nationality, on the forces which produce or weaken it, and on the evils of excessive nationalism. With such questions I am not concerned. Nationality, however produced, is a sense of belonging together, involving a readiness on the part of the members of a state to subordinate their differences to it. It involves something more. It has a connexion with the notion of a distinctive culture—some sort of rough ideal of the kind of common life for which the community stands, which always exists in people's minds as a rough criticism by which political proposals are to be judged. This at least is clear, that where such common understanding and sense of belonging together either does not exist or is overshadowed by other differences, successful democracy is not really possible. If men's sense of economic cleavage is greater than their sense of common nationality, if religious or social or race or colour cleavages are too strong, if there are permanent social minorities, a healthy democracy is so far impossible. Voting in political democracy is successful in so far as the ordinary voter can be relied on to insist on fair play between the different sections and interests in the community, or in so far as the right of a minority to turn itself into a majority is a real and effective right; if these conditions do not exist, voting is only a process of counting heads to save the trouble of breaking them. Representative political democracy involves difference and opposition, but only such difference and opposition as can, as in the discussion in the small religious society, be subordinated to and controlled by the spirit of the whole. It is most interesting to observe how Turkey and China in their effort to become states on the Western model have had deliberately to begin by creating a sense of nationality. They begin indeed by trying to make the spirit of unity so strong that it does not admit of differences. They cannot become democratic states until differences are recognized and maintained alongside of the unity: but the feeling of unity which nationalism strives to create is the indispensable beginning.

These facts suggest that there is something about political democracy, which plays a part analogous to that played in non-political societies by the sense of the meeting or the spirit of the movement. But it is also clear that the purpose of a political society is so different from that, say, of a religious organization, that we cannot get much further until we examine the specific nature of a political organization and its purpose.

LECTURE IV

WE are to ask ourselves in this lecture how far the obvious differences between political democracy and the much more satisfactory democracy of non-political associations are the result of the distinctive purpose and nature of political organization. Something other than the difference in scale between the simple democracy of the congregation and the modern state is needed to account for some at least of the evils and failures of political democracy. Non-political democratic societies feel the difficulties involved in applying on a larger scale the experience of the small society, but they seem on the whole able to surmount these difficulties with comparative success—certainly with much more success than is realized by political democracy. Is it possible that the anti-democrats are right when they say that the failures of political democracy are the result of men acting on the fundamental fallacy that political government can be anything like the government of a non-political society?

We shall probably get most light on the distinctive nature of politics and the relevance of that for democratic problems if we start by considering some of the obvious differences in working and results between political democracy and the democracy of non-political associations. I shall try to formulate some of the dissatisfactions which must have been gathering in the reader's mind as he read the last lecture.

We should probably begin by saying that in actual fact politics tends to be a dirty business. There is always a terrible gulf between the fine and elevating theories about democracy which we read in books on political theory and the actual facts of politics. In actual fact in politics men are obviously very much more 'on the make' than in the non-political democratic societies. Politics seems to be a sphere of contending interests, of men trying to get by political means what they cannot get by their own efforts. It is the scene of a constant struggle for power. No doubt the desire for power is a fundamental fact in human nature and is evident in churches and universities as well as in politics. All kinds of societies suffer from the masterful and ambitious man. But the desire for influence and esteem is comparatively simple and harmless in non-political societies, for the reason that in them power and influence are their own reward. The power which men acquire in non-political societies is on the whole just their influence. But, as Washington said, influence is not government. In politics there is a sharp distinction between men's influence as persons and the official power which they acquire when by means of that influence or in other ways they obtain office. When they are in office, they have beind them a something called the power of the state. That is something for which men strive as they do not ordinarily strive for power in a non-political association, because it is not only its own reward. The power men acquire in a church is after all power exercised in the service of the church. The power men acquire in political office may be turned to the interests of the office holder or his friends. The reason for this difference is of course that the state is a centre of organized force. Government has always behind it more force than men would at any moment give it if they were moved only by persuasion or by their conviction of the soundness of the government's policy. The possibility of the perversion of that official power, the necessity of controlling it in the interests of the community as a whole, are so decisive in the working of political democracy that any attempt to make the government of non-political associations a model for the state is sure to be misleading. No one, for example, would ever have said from a study of non-political democratic societies that government by consent was the essence of democracy. For in a non-political society consent is more or less automatic. If you do not like what a church does you can leave it. You need not nowadays belong to it unless you please. The power of non-democratic business organizations when they are not monopolistic is limited by the fact that we can refuse to buy their wares. We cannot so boycott the state; we have in taxes to pay for its wares whether we like them or not; we have to submit to its orders and rules or suffer. The doctrine that democracy is government by the consent of the governed means simply that the main thing to be done in politics is to give political societies a little of that freedom which the non-political societies get for nothing. So great is the sum with which it has to purchase that freedom that it has no money left for the luxuries of refined democracy in which associations like churches which are born free may well indulge. The discussions on the methods by which non-political societies achieve the truest spirit of democracy are as futile and irrelevant in politics as would be a lecture on the respective advantages of spending money on a Rolls Royce or first editions to men engaged in a struggle for the bare necessities of life.

That is the first objection: The organized force which is the distinctive mark of the state so alters the nature of political problems as to make any analogy between democracy in politics and in non-political societies only misleading.

In the second place, it might well be objected that for all that has been said in favour of discussion the fruitfulness of discussion has very strict limits. This objection may be put in different ways.

There would seem to be some kinds of knowledge to which discussion is essential and other kinds where it counts for very little.

There are a great many things which a government has to do which are hardly matters for discussion at all. They are affairs for experts. They require a knowledge which is mainly acquired by familiarity with and experience of a particular class of problems. This is a familiar distinction in all societies. We all of us know how we have to say from time to time in committees, 'What is the use of our discussing this question? We have not got the knowledge which should form the basis of discussion.' It is the mark of a good chairman to distinguish executive detail from questions of principle, to put before his committee or meeting the principles implied in alternative proposals, and not to waste their time and temper in the dis-

cussion of executive detail. If this distinction between executive detail and questions of principle is true of all societies, it
is especially true of politics. An immense deal of what a
modern government does is as we say a matter of business or
of efficient administration. It is work which not only cannot
be done by a large collection of people, but cannot be done by
ordinary people at all, however few they may be. It is work
which needs special skill and special training, and about that
there is no doubt. The democratic theory that the functions
of government can all be carried on by any average citizen has
done immense harm. It was the basis of the Spoils System in
American politics. In its name inefficiency and ignorance have
been tolerated in politics as they would never be tolerated
in business. The distrust of the expert and the unwillingness
to pay properly for expert services are continually apparent
in trade unionism, and the same distrust has vitiated most
attempts to build up a system of co-operative production.
Political democracy, it is now agreed, requires an expert
civil service, and that civil service cannot be effective unless,
as we say, it is somehow taken out of politics.

What is fundamentally the same objection may be put in
another way, which is perhaps more suggestive. We have
been arguing that most disillusionment with democracy comes
from the contrast of political democracy with the simple
democracy of the small society. Might it not be argued that
it comes as much from men's contrast of the inefficiency of
political government with the efficiency of business administration? It is indeed remarkable how, all through the nineteenth century, as democracy became more and more
triumphant in politics, there was being developed at the same
time a form of organization which was the opposite of
democracy, or, at any rate, very different from it, and in some
ways this new form of government seems to have been much
more successful than democracy. Big business organization
has over-passed the boundaries of political society and produced world wide organizations with comparative ease, while
it has taken a world war to produce an international political

organization even as comparatively ineffective as the League of Nations. We are often told nowadays that power has already passed into the hands of the large business organizations. It is they who really govern the world and all that democratic political organization can do is to register or perhaps hamper slightly their decisions. If you want to get things done in the world, we are told, get power in business administration. If you only want to talk about getting them done, go into politics. A recent writer has elaborated this theme in a book with a significant title, *The Passing of Politics*. The old political order, it is admitted, has not yet entirely passed away. It still presents a pretentious façade to the public. It still makes some show of power and it can still help or hinder the real wielders of power enough for them to have to pay some attention to it, but its power is passing away and we shall soon all recognize what a sham it has become.

It is interesting to observe the comparative atrophy in business of its one democratic element, the meeting of stockholders. The organization of a joint stock company may have an appearance of democracy, especially where the stock is not held in large blocks, but it is widely distributed. Recent writers have made much of the argument that capitalism has largely changed its character because stocks are so widely held that the ordinary working man is himself a capitalist. But joint stock companies are not more than nominally democracies. Their meetings of stock-holders have little power, and the atrophy of the stock-holders' meeting suggests that the democratic element in joint stock companies has proved inefficient, that the meeting of stock-holders has very little effect on the working of a company, and that what effect it has is bad.

Of course there is another side to all this. There is a great school of thought which argues that we shall never get rid of industrial unrest until we have somehow democratized industry. But the extraordinary growth of non-democratic business organizations is at least a prima facie argument against democracy. Modern business organization depends on specialization, and is not democracy in some sense the denial of specialization? Is there no meaning in the demand of which we hear so much for a business administration in government; must we not admit that there must be *something* in a demand so insistent. Should we not ask rather whether there is anything to be said against it?

The objection may be put in yet another way. Modern democracy came, we have said, from the Independents, the Anabaptists, and the Quakers, the Protestant sects who believed in one form or other in the doctrine of the Inner Light; but these sects tended to be Quietist enough to assert that religion is not really concerned with the things of this world, certainly not with more than the conscience of the individual. When the Inner Light tells some people how other people should act or should be made to act, it is apt to be regarded as a nuisance. 'The principle of the Inward Light', said Dr. Johnson, 'to which some Methodists pretend, is totally incompatible with political and social security.' It looks as though democratic discussion could be valuable in one of two sets of circumstances; either in a very simple society where the problems discussed are problems with which all men have some familiarity and to the solution of which therefore their special experience can make a special contribution; or in religious societies where men are not concerned with everyday problems at all but with sharing with one another the message of God to their individual souls. Politics as we know it is, in contrast with these two spheres, occupied with things of the middle distance. In politics we are concerned with practical dealings with other men, but with other men with whom we do not stand in personal relations and about whom we know little or nothing. We think of them by means of what Mr. Walter Lippmann calls stereotypes, formulas and abstractions with very little reality about them. In the last lecture we were discussing the difficulties arising from the growth in the numbers of those who should take part in discussion. But is not the real difficulty in democratic politics that the subjects of discussion, the matters with which the modern state has to deal, have far outgrown the individual's knowledge and consciousness, so that in most matters which he is asked to decide he is not and cannot be informed enough to have any real opinion, and so can make no real contribution? Aristotle long ago in discussing the nature of deliberation said it was not possible for a Greek to deliberate how the Scythians should be governed. It is just as impossible for us to deliberate in any real sense of the word about the government of present day Scythia, but our government, for which we are responsible, has got to take some attitude towards the present government of Russia. Is not the voter, and indeed the legislator, in modern democracy continually being asked nowadays to choose between two alternatives neither of which he understands?

We hear a great deal in recent sociological writing about the irrationality of human nature. Why is it that it has been left to modern psychology to make this portentous discovery that man is not a rational animal? Is not the explanation that he is as rational as he ever was, and he goes on displaying his rationality wherever he is dealing with problems which are within his grasp and his knowledge, but that modern democracy is continually asking him to decide upon problems which are quite outside his knowledge, which he is, therefore, bound to decide on irrational grounds?

Or again, it may be objected that the suggestion made at the end of the last lecture that nationality plays in politics the part which is played in the tiny democracy by the sense of the meeting arouses some disquieting reflections. In face of the facts, in face of the persistent danger of nationalism to the peace of the world, is it really possible to suggest that nationalism is but the distemper or measles of nationality; it has to be, but it is got over and will then settle down into a sober and rational thing called nationality? Must we not admit that the difficulty is that the state does not seem as such to have that lively acceptance of its common purpose which can on the whole be found in other associations? Churches are voluntary organizations and therefore pre-

sumably, if people take no interest or do not believe in their
purpose they need not belong to them or may leave them.
They may therefore take for granted that all their members
believe in that purpose and are animated by a collective spirit.
Political organizations are, as we have seen, compulsory and
have to apply to all who live in a given territory, whatever
their feelings or purposes may be. One of the outstanding
difficulties in politics is the general indifference of the great
mass of the voters. The ordinary man regards politics as a
nuisance, something with which he would much rather have
nothing to do, taking part in which is at best a disagreeable
duty. Must we admit that in face of this general indifference
democracy is only possible if men are whipped up into a state
of unnatural and irrational excitement, that that is the only
kind of emotional bond which can make men feel enough
interest in politics to make democracy in the lest possible?
Perhaps there is more method than we admitted in the second
lecture in the apparent madness of these processes of producing mass enthusiasm or collective drunkenness which
characterizes so much in modern democracy. If there were
no party conflicts and no mass meetings and no collective
enthusiasm, should we not all be so bored with politics that
we should not vote? And would not that mean, does it not
mean that in that general indifference those who have a
genuine interest in politics, not for their or the public health,
but for what they can get out of it, get away with the spoils?
Why does the Press deal in scares and rows? Why does it
seem to be like a little boy egging on a dog fight, except that
scares and rows and clashes are news because they are exciting,
and agreement and serious discussion and constructive proposals are not news because we find them comparatively
boring? And is not the moral of all this that we can produce in
politics something corresponding to the sense of the meeting
at the expense of its not being sense, but nonsense and
dangerous nonsense at that? And must we not go further
and ask what is the use of our being offered nationality as
a substitute for the sense of the meeting when by this time

our problems are international, when what we want more than anything else is a sense of world citizenship? But what kind of drive for the ordinary voter is there behind the sense of world citizenship? We could probably train up an international civil service, a staff of trained experts who would look at world problems from a world point of view. That is being already done in the Secretariat of the League of Nations at Geneva. What a refreshing and fine and altogether admirable attitude towards world problems do you not find there. What a contrast that is with the atmosphere pervading the debates on foreign policy in any political assembly. Are not these experts and their sort the people to govern the world? Would you not rather that your foreign affairs were governed from Williamstown than from Washington? If we could get rid of this foolish belief in democracy and set our minds on selecting and training a skilled professional governmental service, should we not all be better off?

These seem to me to be formidable objections. We may perhaps summarize them in the general statement that in our attempt to understand politics by the light of non-political democracy we forgot that the state depends upon force and is therefore the scene of conflict for power; that it is a compulsory organization that applies to every one and not only to those who, like the members of a religious organization, are animated by a common spirit or purpose, and thirdly that the work it has got to do is of so complicated and technical a nature that it needs above all technical and expert knowledge and that therefore the proper model for the state is not the democratic religious society but the non-democratic business organization.

It will be clear, I think, that the main source of these objections which we have been considering is the fact that the state for its purposes uses force or compulsion. It will be well therefore to consider a little what part the element of force plays in the state and how greatly the presence of that element distinguishes the state from other associations.

We are sometimes told that the state rests on force. That

is not true. It is, I think, true that the possession and use of organized force is the distinctive mark of the state. The state indeed insists on maintaining a monopoly of such force. But its main purpose in doing so is to ensure that individuals and other organizations do not, as the saying goes, take the law into their own hands. The use of the state's force is to deny the use of force to individuals and organizations in settling their disputes, or to insist that disputes should be settled by legal process. Its business is to keep other organizations voluntary, to see that they do depend upon consent. A state which permits private warfare is not doing what it ought to do. But this means that the organized force of the state is as it were a force to end the use of force and establish the rule of law, and the state possesses and uses organized force because most people in the state are determined that the rule of law shall prevail, are prepared to insist on a peaceful and constitutional settlement of differences. So far then from the state's resting on force, the state's organized force rests on men's confidence in government and their belief in law.

It is also clear that the state can only enforce obedience to law if the laws are such that most people do not want to break them. Let a state, however powerful, pass a law which the mass of the people do not respect or to which a considerable minority violently object, and the enforcement of the law will be very difficult if not impossible. There is no need to insist on that at the present time.

This is but to restate at greater length T. H. Green's dictum that will, not force, is the basis of the state. But if that is true, if the existence of government rests on people's confidence it it or sense of the need for it, if laws are enforceable only if the people are behind them, why does the government need organized force, why need laws be enforced? Is it not a paradox to say at the same time that will, not force, is the basis of the state, and that the possession of organized force is the distinctive mark of the state? The answer is that government and the organized force of government in the support of law are *possible* because most people give government their loyal and unforced support and because *most* people *mostly* wish to obey the law. But the acts of government and laws have to apply to everybody all the time. Most people usually wish to obey the law. Everybody has to obey it always. An organized force is at the disposal of government behind the law because most people usually want to obey the law. It is necessary to fill up the margin between most people and everybody, between usually and always.

Most of us would usually obey the law if there were no sanctions behind it, but most of us would occasionally break it and in these matters example is contagious. We most of us, for example, pay our taxes with comparative cheerfulness and from a sense of duty; but if we knew that taxpaying were left to a citizen's sense of duty and that we had to pay higher taxes than were our share because other citizens with less sense of duty than ourselves refused to pay, and that if we refused to pay, all that would happen would be that citizens with a still higher sense of duty than ourselves would have to bear the whole burden, we should all, to say the least of it, find our sense of duty considerably strained; and if we resisted the strain and went on paying our taxes, knowing that their steady increase was due to the fact that other people in increasing numbers were evading taxation, we should feel a great sense of injustice and should demand that all should be compelled to pay their share of taxation. The justification of force is that there are some things which have got to be done by everybody or for everybody if they are to be done at all. The state is a compulsory organization in the sense that it uses compulsion and force, because it is a compulsory organization in the other sense that its rules necessarily apply to all persons living in a given territory whether they want to support the state or not.

We may see now that the existence of the margin, or, as the economists would call it, 'the lag', between most people usually obeying which makes government possible and all people always having to obey which makes force necessary, explains how the organized force which a government uses may be perverted. If most people did not have confidence in government, there would be no government. But people's confidence in government is, so to speak, capitalized in the organized force which is at the government's disposal, and a government can for a time live on its capital or act in a way which does not increase or maintain the people's confidence in government. If it goes on living on its capital long enough, it will suffer the fate which usually follows on such behaviour. People will cease to obey it and then there will be a revolution. Only very stupid governments bring about revolution, but all governments live on their capital from time to time; presuming on the fact that the great mass of people will submit to a government behaving in a way which they dislike or disapprove because they recognize that a bad government is better than no government, and are not able or not prepared to make the effort necessary to make that bad government a better government. In the same way people adopt and support a certain form of government, a democratic constitution for example, because they expect it to produce the kind of governmental action and the kind of laws of which they will approve. If it persistently fails to do this, the constitution will be changed; but even a good constitution will sometimes produce bad results and bad laws, and the bad laws will be acquiesced in for the sake of the general goodness of the constitution. If a government persistently and obstinately disregards the public service or what people will stand, it will in time come to a bad end. But if it is not unrighteous overmuch and exercises moderation in wickedness, it may flourish like a green bay tree, unless its citizens have a high degree of public spirit and public vigilance.

All this is a long way of saying that no government, however democratic, can be founded on consent, in the sense of particularized consent, and that any government, however undemocratic, is founded on consent in the sense of generalized consent, and the aim of a good constitution is to ensure that government should have the power to do what the country requires and yet should be incapable of using that power for perverted ends. If we can get this idea of universal consent out of our minds and consider the matter as a practical problem, we shall see that there are roughly two ways of securing our aims. We may either try to put in power persons who are not likely to abuse their power or we may take means to ensure that if they do abuse their power they shall be pulled up. Both means are probably necessary, but for some reason the second device is usually supposed to be more democratic than the other. Annual elections, checks, and balances, and the recall and the referendum are devices of the second sort. But it is now, I think, recognized that if you set up a government in which men will immediately be hauled up if they do wrong, they may very easily be hauled up if they do right and you will not get a government capable of doing anything at all. The cry for annual Parliaments has ceased to be a democratic slogan. The British people had the privilege of having two general elections in one year lately and their vote on the second occasion was largely influenced by their determination that such a thing should not happen again. Somehow we must manage to get a government which is more likely than not to do what will be approved. How is that done? Parliamentary and Presidential government represent two different ways of handling the problem. The Parliamentary solution is to have only one lot of people—the representatives—elected, and to make all the other holders of office, the executive, the civil service, and the judiciary responsible to them; the Presidential plan is to have direct election of the different holders of office and to determine their relations to one another by a constitution. I do not wish to discuss the respective merits of these two plans, but to notice that the advantages and disadvantages of popular election vary very much with the work which the different kinds of officials have to do, and to insist that we should face this honestly. We should recognize that government is there to carry out the purpose of the community, that it must be made both sensitive to that purpose and efficient, and we

shall thus find that, its purpose being complex, it needs
different kinds of servants, and there may be different ways
of appointing them which will all be equally democratic if
they fulfil the two conditions of sensitiveness and efficiency.
That and not pedantic uniformity is what democracy demands.
Everyone would agree that in a democracy representatives
should be elected, that there must be an organ of government
necessarily in touch with and responsive to the wishes and
experiences of the ordinary person. Both systems agree in
thinking that the executive should also be either by direct
election or by immediate responsibility to directly elected
persons sensitive to public opinion. Both systems, on the
other hand, now agree that there should be a permanent civil
service, that it should not be directly elected but chosen for
professional and technical service. Its concern is with means
and not with ends. Its business is to put at the disposal of
the policy determining organ exact and impartial knowledge
and expert service. The expert civil servant is indispensable,
but indispensable as a servant, not as a master of policy.
There is no such agreement as to how judges ought to be
appointed, but it would probably be agreed that there are
great disadvantages in making judges too directly sensitive
to public opinion, and they can, it is clear, be kept from
abusing their power by quite different means. The judge is
kept from imposing his personal will by the fact that he has
to interpret the law, and his whole training, his professional
honour, and the public opinion of his profession make him
the servant of the law. These sanctions are likely to make
him a much better judge, a much better servant of the purpose
of the community than are the more democratic devices of
direct popular election and a short term of office.

The moral of all this surely is that in a democratic government we need compulsion in order to carry out the purpose
of the state, that the purpose of that compulsion is to insist
on a legal and constitutional method of settlement of differences and rivalries within the community, and that the
problem of how to keep governmental power from being

perverted to private ends can be and is solved in different ways.

The attempt to make consent to the acts of government as particularized as possible by universal popular election and a short term of office for all officials has clearly broken down when applied to the skilled civil service and is felt to have great disadvantages when applied to judges. But the universal agreement that law making assemblies should be popularly elected implies a belief that the purpose of government is such that it not only needs skilled and efficient instruments but persons peculiarly sensible to and understanding of the lives and problems and opinions of the ordinary members of the community.

If this is right, we may, I think, maintain that our first main objection is answered. The fact that the purpose of the state needs force behind it makes political government more complicated than is the government of a non-political association. It introduces new dangers against which precautions have to be taken; but those precautions are all to ensure that force is the servant and not the master of politics; that the state should not be just the conflict of forces, but the means of achieving a purpose in which special skill and knowledge and leadership are subordinated to a purpose, the proper understanding and direction of which needs understanding of the aim and purposes of the ordinary members of the community. But that is surely in principle what characterized the purpose of the non-political association. Let us see now whether our examination of the other objections will give a different result.

LECTURE V

THE second objection which was formulated in the last lecture was concerned with the limits of fruitful discussion. To one of the forms in which it was put the end of the last lecture has already suggested an answer. It is clear that some of the knowledge required in government is of a kind not gained by discussion but by special skill and study. Government cannot get on without experts, and popular election is not the best way of choosing experts. Most men would agree that democratic government cannot hope to be efficient without a permanent skilled civil service, and that that civil service should be out of politics. The ordinary means of achieving that result is to have the responsible heads of departments not experts but laymen—politicians, in the good sense of that much-abused term. They are responsible for the acts of their expert subordinates, either to the legislative assembly on the Parliamentary system or to the head of the executive on the Presidential. For our purpose it is important to note that while no one wants the civil service to be as sensitive to public opinion as the representative ought to be, there are disadvantages in a civil service being too insensitive to public opinion. Civil servants have got to be impartial—to be able to serve this or that policy determined by their political chiefs, and yet have understanding of and sympathy with the ordinary life of the people. Otherwise they may easily become a bureaucracy. The various ways in which this sensitiveness of the second degree, as we may call it, can be achieved need not concern us. The fact that question time in the House of Commons has been called the corner-stone of British liberties may suggest the sort of answer that might be given to that problem. The important point for the theory of democracy is that this sensitiveness is required. For it will put us in the way to answer the second form of the objection we are considering—the suggestion that the proper model for government is not the religious democratic society but the undemocratic business organization.

We had the beginnings of an answer to that objection in the last lecture, when we noticed that the public have usually this automatic check on business organizations—that they need not buy their goods. That of course is not always true. But it is interesting to observe that our satisfaction with business in preference to democratic organization has always waned when the business organization becomes monopolistic. Then the uncontrolled government of the business organization is the last thing we want. As the growth of large-scale organization in industry has made much business semi-monopolistic, the necessity of the regulation of industry by the democratic state has become more and more taken for granted. There is still great difference of opinion as to the proper extent and methods of that regulation, but general agreement that in so far as industry or business becomes monopolistic, in so far it has to be regulated in the public interest.

Business organization was formerly allowed to develop almost entirely independently of political control, because it was not regarded as a form of government at all. For under a perfect system of free exchange the economic system might be and was regarded as concerned simply with the satisfaction of wants. It was not concerned with why individuals wanted what they did, or whether they ought to want different things: that was the business of morality. Nor was it concerned with seeing that the effective demand of individuals was equal: that was the concern of politics. Economic organization took wants and effective demand for granted and increased supply and satisfaction. It left individuals and their wants where it found them. It did not control or govern people at all—only made satisfaction of wants immensely more effective. It was to be an instrument, and nothing but an instrument, and its watchword was efficiency.

That is the theoretical social justification of *laissez-faire*, and if the facts were anything like the theory (or so far as the facts are like the theory) it is a sound justification. But these neat and clear-cut distinctions of means and ends, instruments and purposes, usually break down in practice. Man has a way of becoming enslaved to his own instruments, and of getting so occupied with the means of life that he forgets the end. This great economic instrument of modern life did not by any means leave society where it found it, only making it more efficient. It profoundly transformed its whole structure. It does not simply take wants for granted. It spends much of its time in stimulating wants. Furthermore and above all, it found that the discipline and organization of men by men was a potent instrument of production; and its structure became something very different from a free exchange of services.

But as it became gradually clear that these things were happening, that the economic instrument was becoming the master of society, a persistent demand arose that the economic instrument should be consciously controlled by society in so far as it was not automatically controlled by all the individuals constituting society. That is the principle behind the regulation of economic organization by the state. As it became clear that the structure of business organization was coming to involve government, the demand arose that that government should not be despotic but democratic. The true solution of the problem of the government of industry has not yet been discovered. It is in process of being worked out. But we can say that it is becoming more and more of a commonplace that business has somehow to be made responsible to the democratic state, and that its internal constitution has got to become and is becoming more democratic.

But to admit all this is only to repeat a point made in the last lecture—that political democracy is necessary to give monopolistic and compulsory associations something corresponding to the freedom which all voluntary associations enjoy automatically. Is not that exactly what the above argument implies? In so far as business and economic organization can remain really on a basis of consent and free contract, in so far no government or democratic control is necessary. In so far as it becomes monopolistic and compulsory, some element of public consent becomes necessary to replace the private consent which has disappeared. There is need for some democratic machinery to keep the efficient expert straight, to keep him as an instrument and not as a master. As we said in discussing the place of voting in the public meeting, voting is wanted when things go wrong, and the possibility of voting to prevent things from going wrong. But, it may be asked, how is this relevant to the objection as to the limits of frutiful discussion? Of course discussion and criticism are important in business as they are elsewhere, but only the discussion and criticism of men who, if not technicians, are business experts. The ordinary man does not want to have his economic wants settled by discussion. He desires to have his power of individual demand—his private consent—safeguarded. Does not this suggest that we want efficient specialists checked by a stockholders' meeting enlarged to include not only stockholders but representatives of the general public and of employees? The model for democratic organization will not be business organization as it exists at present, but rather that type of business organization which is being evolved to correct the monopolistic and compulsory character of existing business organization. The purpose of government on this argument is in principle an economic purpose. Its function is to enable men better to achieve their purposes. Its purpose therefore is strictly instrumental to individual purposes. Its most typical function then is traffic control. The aim of traffic control and regulations is not to tell people where they are to go, but by common regulation to enable individuals to go more efficiently and freely where they want to go. Society as a whole, in this view, has no real purpose, and therefore there is nothing and ought to be nothing corresponding to the sense of the meeting or the spirit of the movement.

Now there is obviously a good deal of truth in this position. Many of the activities of government are directed to seeing that individuals are efficiently supplied with what as individuals they want. There are things which governments do in some countries which are done by what is called private enterprise in others, and the choice between these two methods of conducting, say, a telephone service, is surely one of the respective efficiency of the services rendered. Most (though not all) of the functions of city government are of this sort. The city government can take for granted that there are certain things which all its citizens want—streets, lighting, drainage, water, and so on—and its business is to supply them as economically and efficiently as possible ; and that can be done by an efficient business administration, kept straight by the general voting control of the public.

But clearly all the functions of government are not of this sort. There are some things which an economic organization can take for granted with which a community must concern itself. The satisfaction of individual wants may and does have reactions on the community as a whole. The distribution of effective demand is not the concern of the economic organization, but it is a matter of great concern to the community. The fact that men are prepared to pay for something is not sufficient guarantee that the satisfaction of the demand for it is socially necessary, nor is the fact that individuals are not prepared to pay for something evidence that that thing is not wanted by the community. All modern democratic countries discourage in various degrees of discouragement the demand for alcohol and certain kinds of drugs, and encourage with special endowments and otherwise the demand for education. The type of education so encouraged will not be necessarily that for which individual people are prepared to pay. It will be that which is judged most valuable for the community as a whole. This does not imply that endowment of education means that people in power determine that it is good for other people to have education, or that licensing laws are passed by people who want to prevent other people from drinking. That of course does happen in much legislation. We are all apt to

Compound for sins we are inclined to
By damning those we have no mind to.

But educational endowment and licensing laws may perfectly
well be passed by the votes of ordinary people who would
not make the necessary effort to get education or deny
themselves liquor in their individual action, but who have
a higher standard of values for themselves and others as
members of the community.

I am unjust, but I can strive for justice.
    My life's unkind, but I can vote for kindness.
I, the unloving, say life should be lovely ;
    I, that am blind, cry out against my blindness.

Man is a curious brute—he pets his fancies—
    Fighting mankind to win sweet luxury,
So he will be, tho law be clear as crystal,
    Tho all men plan to live in harmony.

Come, let us vote against our human nature,
    Crying to God in all the polling places
To heal our everlasting sinfulness,
    And make us sages with transfigured faces.[1]

Legislation and government action are concerned not only
with satisfying individual demand but with moral issues,
with upholding a certain standard and manner of life. Without such a conception of the kind of life to be encouraged
and the kind to be discouraged—without a pervading notion
of what a country stands for—there would be no standard
of legislation. This standard of the conception of the good
life of the community is never clearly grasped: it is differently
interpreted by different people and by different parties.
Think how nineteenth-century Liberalism and Conservatism
in England both express something characteristic of and
essential to English life. Read the debate between Senator
Borah and President Nicholas Murray Butler on the Eigh-
teenth Amendment, and notice how characteristic of what is
best and most influential in American public opinion each of

[1] Nicholas Vachel Lindsay, *Why I Voted the Socialist Ticket*.

these conflicting presentments is. But complex and vague as that standard is, it is very real: it expresses itself in a country's laws, in its public policy, in its system of education, and in its institutions.

This outstanding fact about the state—that its legislation and much of its activities appeal to and seek to maintain a certain way of life—has been often taken to mean that the state's business is to make men good: it is an institution for the realization of morality. It was thus that Plato and Aristotle regarded the state. And if that is so it seems more difficult than ever to defend democracy. For do we not all recognize the existence of moral geniuses—of men of commanding moral insight? If the state is an instrument of morality, should it not be an instrument in the hands of Plato's philosopher king, or be ruled by its saints? There is a passage in the Protagoras where Socrates puts very searchingly the fundamental quarrel between this view of the state and democracy.

'When we are met together in the assembly and the matter in hand relates to building, the builders are summoned as advisors; when the question is one of shipbuilding, then the shipwrights; and the other like arts which they think capable of being taught and learned. And if some person offers to give them advice who is not supposed by them to have any skill in the art, even though he be goodlooking and rich and noble, they will not listen to him but laugh and hoot at him, until he is clamoured down and retires. . . . But when the question is an affair of state, then everybody is free to have a say— carpenters, tinker, collier, sailor, passenger; rich and poor, high and low—anyone who likes gets up and none reproaches him, as in the former case, with not having learned, and having no teacher and yet giving advice.'

Plato developd the implications of this criticism in his doctrine that there can be no salvation to states until they are ruled by men with true understanding of the ends or purposes of life. The same view of the state was implicit in the Calvinism of Geneva. Calvinism was not democratic.

It demanded the rule of the saints. If moral knowledge and insight are to be in authority, if the state is to do moral tasks, ought it not to be ruled by moral experts?

It is no real answer to this to say, however true it may be, that moral genius may appear without education or rank or any other socially prized qualification. That is an argument for the Calvinist rule of the saints as against Plato's demand for the rule of the philosopher, but it is not an argument for democracy. Democracy rests on the principle, not that all men's views on what are right and wrong are of equal value, nor on the denial of the existence of saints and prophets, but on the doctrine that compulsory morality is a contradiction in terms. Its prophets are Roger Williams and Oliver Cromwell. Döllinger, in a lecture on Founders of Religion, has these significant words on Cromwell:

'He was the first among the mighty men of the world to set up one special religious principle, and to enforce it so far as in him lay: . . . the principle of liberty of conscience and the repudiation of religious coercion. It must be clearly understood how great the gulf is which divides the holders of this principle from those who reject it, both in faith and morals. He who is convinced that right and duty require him to coerce other people into a life of falsehood . . . belongs to an essentially different religion from one who recognizes in the inviolability of conscience a human right guaranteed by religion itself, and has different notions of God, of man's relation to God, and of man's obligations to his fellows. . . . It is only of this one doctrine that Cromwell can be called the prophet, for he adhered upon all other points to the tenets of the Independents; yet the doctrine of liberty of conscience has struck deeper into the course of events and has had a larger share in the development of modern religious feeling than a dozen dogmas, sprung from theological schools, that affect merely the intellect and not the soul—that is, the will— of the believer. The Constitution of the United States of America has been built up upon Cromwell's doctrine; and there is every prospect that, as one of the great powers of the world, it will leave its mark upon the future of mankind.'

This does not mean that prophets and saints are not to guide and illumine our moral lives—but that they are to do it by persuasion and example and not by force. The state needs the church, or rather all kinds of voluntary moral organizations, and must take them for granted, and its business is to safeguard by harmonious regulation the rich various life of voluntary associations in the state. Its purpose, in Bosanquet's phrase, is to hinder hindrances to the good life. That implies our statement from Colonel Rainboro that the poorest he that is in England has a life to live as the richest he, supplemented and completed by the knowledge that men and women live their own life, not in abstract isolation, but in all kinds of institutions and associations; that the best society is that which increases spontaneity and life and variety; and that that is not primarily done by the state but by all this rich complex of voluntary associations. The end of the state's compulsion is to give room for liberty—but not just for the independent liberty of individuals but for the kind of freedom and liberty which are possible only in social life. That the state cannot itself produce, but it can do an immense deal to foster the forces which do produce it, and by its power of regulation and adjustment it can keep this spontaneous life from losing itself in anarchy.

When modern political theory tried to give an intelligible account of the nineteenth-century democratic state, is started with the conception borrowed from Rousseau that democracy was government by or in accordance with the general will, and that was taken at first to mean roughly the same as government by public opinion or the will of the people. But Rousseau, in spite of his tendency to identify that with government by consent, had made a distinction between the general will and what he called the will of all. All those who reflected on the principles of democracy agreed that there was something—ordinarily called the general will—to which votes and legislation were trying to give expression. But as the political theorists tried to give this conception of general will more depth and reality, they distinguished it more and more from anything which could be called consent or any explicit expression of will, till in the classical account of general will in Bosanquet's *Philosophical Theory of the State* the general will—the standard by which legislation should be guided—the ideal which public discussion and voting are trying to make explicit—becomes the whole life of society. I quote from an article in which I have tried to summarize the kernel of Bosanquet's doctrine:

'What Bosanquet seems to have done in his account of the general will is to have developed a hint of Rousseau's into a masterly account of the elaborate system of institutions and mutual relations which go to make up the life of society, to have insisted on its complexity and vitality and richness, its transcendence of what any one individual can conceive or express, and then to have said: *That* in all its elaborateness and multifariousness *is* the state; it is nothing less than that; and that is the standard of legislation and of what we ordinarily call state action. The business of politics is to take this elaborate complex of institutions for granted and to seek to remove disharmonies which are thwarting its life and checking its vitality. The state in the narrow political sense is the hinderer of hindrances. The aim of its compulsion and the criterion of the success of that compulsion is the setting free of the spontaneity which is inherent in the life of society. Political machinery, general elections, legislatures, judicians, and executors are endeavouring or ought to be endeavouring to express the spirit of a common social life.'

Now it is clear that if this common life is to be the standard of legislation we need in the legislator and the government an understanding of it, and that understanding can only be obtained if that common life finds explicit expression in discussion in which all concerned in that common life—individuals and voluntary associations—take part. Without that the most expert legislator cannot know where the adjustment and regulation of government is necessary ('only the wearer knows where the shoe pinches'), and he cannot know what effect his legislation and enactments will have.

A second-class law obeyed is better than a first-class law disobeyed. What is needed, and what is most difficult, is to combine the technical knowledge of the expert with the practical experience and understanding of the common life of the ordinary public. The expert has to be sensitive to public opinion; the ordinary man has somehow to discuss with some understanding of what the experts' proposals amount to. Democracy assumes for its success an educated public: but if all the voluntary associations are centres of education in thinking publicly the task of public education is not quite so hopeless as it would otherwise be.

It follows from this view of the function of the state that politics are a secondary matter. Plato said long ago that the state would be well ruled only when its rulers had a life better than the political one. If the purpose of the state's force is to guard and maintain and harmonize a common life, the greater the strength and spontaneity of that common life the more necessary but the easier will be the task of the state— the more necessary because vigorous and spontaneous life produces clashes of interests, new disharmonies, all kinds of possibilities of conflict; the easier because the more real and active the common life, the more real will public opinion be, and the easier the expression of the general will.

We can perhaps now see at least the beginning of an answer to the most serious of the objections raised in the last lecture—the objection that the ordinary voter regards politics with indifference, and is only whipped up to vote by forms of collective excitement such as nationalism or party enthusiasm. These artificial and irrational forms of uniting men are necessary just so far as they are not naturally united in sharing in a wide common culture and participating in a common life where there are no cultural enclaves, where there is real spiritual communication among groups, where in fact the smaller groupings unite and do not divide. Where that is not the case, in a community with cultural or economic or religious barriers, only some cause which enlists strong irrational excitement can force men together to the necessary

degree to get the work of government done. In that sense
it is true that nationalism is as it were the measles of nationality. Nations are made nations usually by strong external
forces. To-day, when men give at least a lip service to
democratic equality, the unity which is necessary in a society
which has not a democratic social structure is given by an
irrational nationalism—as in Italy, Russia, or China. Mere
politics (that means the organization with force behind it)
has got to do the work which in a real democratic society is
done by voluntary cultural associations. The state has to
become a church, with bad results for both state and church.
For nationalism, one of the most powerful religions in the
world to-day, is 'a very degraded form of polytheism'.

It follows in the same way that in so far as our non-political
associations are undemocratic—in so far as their members
are not inspired by a common purpose but kept together by
force—our membership of them, instead of being a training
in a larger citizenship, will teach us to expect in politics a
similar conflict for power. So long as our industrial system
remains—what it is largely now—a sphere of unresolved
conflict, so long will each of the parties to that conflict try
to use the state's force for its own purposes, and the Marxian
doctrine of the class war be partially true.

But we may make our non-political associations really
democratic, and in so far as we do that, not only are they
schools of citizenship, but they also help to form and make
public opinion—to spread among us all that kind of understanding of the common life of society and of the place in it
of its various forms of social activity which will make a
really democratic political government possible. We cannot,
I think, ever make our political government, *considered in
itself*, really representative. The scale on which it has to
operate is too vast—its units, the constituencies, are, if taken
in themselves, too big and far too little informed by any
public spirit to be really democratic. But if a vigorous non-
political democratic life exists, the political machinery may
harmonize and co-ordinate all that partial focussing of public

opinion which the non-political associations perform. There can be, and there is increasingly coming to be, a vast deal of public discussion and political education focussed by universities, by churches, and by all kinds of cultural associations.

This may all seem a far cry from what happens to-day. Politics is still largely a scene of conflicts for power and of irrational enthusiasms. No democratic political machinery, however well devised, can in itself make it different. Against the perversion and abuse of political power by powerful interests the individual is singularly helpless. Improvised and *ad hoc* reform associations are not much more effective. Only associations which exist for their own purposes and are yet concerned for the public welfare as a whole (such as churches can be and sometimes are) can do what is wanted. But it is astonishing how much is already done by non-political associations like churches and universities to create a disinterested and real public opinion.

Complacent optimism about democracy has done much harm in the past, but the disillusioned scepticism which has taken its place is worse. There are all kinds of grounds for alarm, but there are as many grounds for rational hope. We have suffered in the past from making democracy into a dogma, in the sense of thinking of it as something magical, exempt from the ordinary laws which govern human nature. The conversion of principles into magical dogmas has the same effect in politics as it has in religion. The magic that cannot be believed is accepted till it is found out, and then the true principle on which it was based is abandoned along with it. Democracy implies faith, but a reasoned faith.